炒锅

CHINESE COOKING

ANNABEL JACKSON

CHINESE COOKING

Love Food ® is an imprint of Parragon Books Ltd

Parragon
Queen Street House
4 Queen Street
Bath BA1 1HE, UK

Copyright © Parragon Books Ltd 2004

Love Food ® and the accompanying heart device is a trademark of Parragon
Books Ltd

Created and produced by The Bridgewater Book Company Ltd.

Project Editor Emily Casey Bailey

Project Designer Michael Whitehead

Editor Kay Halsey

Photography Laurie Evans

Home Economist Annie Rigg

Recipe Translations Kathy Leung

Location photography Karen Thomas (2, 12, 16, 19, 25, 35, 49, 77, 100,
111, 144, 147, 235, 240, 248), Olga Vitale Picture Collection (82, 110, 170)

Front cover photography Mike Hemsley at Walter Gardiner

ISBN: 978-1-4075-4920-0

Printed in China

NOTES FOR THE READER

- This book uses both imperial, metric, or US cup measurements. Follow the
  same units of measurement throughout; do not mix imperial and metric.

- All spoon measurements are level: teaspoons are assumed to be
  5 ml, and tablespoons are assumed to be 15 ml.

- Unless otherwise stated, milk is assumed to be whole, eggs and individual
  vegetables such as potatoes are medium, and pepper is freshly ground black
  pepper.

- Recipes using raw or very lightly cooked eggs should be avoided by infants,
  the elderly, pregnant women, convalescents, and anyone with a chronic
  condition.

- The times given are an approximate guide only. Preparation times differ
  according to the techniques used by different people and the cooking times
  may also vary from those given.

contents

Introduction   8
In the Chinese Kitchen   28
In the Chinese Pantry   28

Appetizers, Snacks & Soups   32
Spring Rolls *Cheun Gyun*   40
Vegetarian Spring Rolls *Sou Choi Cheun Gyun*   43
Soft-wrapped Pork and Shrimp Rolls *Chung Sik Yut Naam Cheun Gyun*   44
Shrimp Toasts *Ha Do Si*   46
Scallion Cakes *Chung Yau Beng*   47
Onion Pancakes *Heung Chung Bok Beng*   49
Jiaozi *Gaau Ji*   50
Dumplings in a Cold Spicy Sauce *Choi Yuk Wun Tun*   53
Soy Chicken Wings *Si Yau Gai Yik*   56
Whitebait with Green Chili *Laat Mei Baat Faan Yu*   57
Tea-scented Eggs *Cha Yip Daan*   58
Pickled Baby Cucumbers *Leung Bun Siu Wong Gwa*   59
Marinated Soybeans *Leung Bun Wong Dau*   60
Beancurd and Bean Sprout Soup *Nga Choi Dau Fu Tong*   61
Congee with Fish Fillet *Yu Pin Juk*   62
Hot-and-sour Soup *Syun Laat Tong*   65
Crab and Corn Soup *Hai Yung Suk Mai Gang*   66
Sichuan Pumpkin Soup *Chyun Mei Naam Gwa Tong*   67
Ground Beef and Cilantro Soup *Ngau Sung Yin Sai Tong*   69
Tomato Soup with Conpoy *Yui Chyu Faan Ke Tong*   70
Whole Chicken Soup *Wun Teui Ching Gai Tong*   71
Won Ton Soup *Wun Tun Tong*   72

Fish & Seafood   74
Cantonese Steamed Fish *Ching Jing Yu*   82
Deep-fried River Fish with Chili Bean Sauce *Dau Faan Yu*   85
Five-willow Fish *M Lau Yu*   86
Fried Fish with Pine Kernels *Chung Ji Yu*   89
Chilies Stuffed with Fish Paste *Yu Yuk Yeung Laat Jin*   90
Steamed Sole with Black Bean Sauce *Si Jap Jin Taap Sa*   92
Drunken Shrimp *Jeui Ha*   93
Shrimp Fu Yung *Fu Yung Ha*   96
Wok-fried Jumbo Shrimp in Spicy Sauce *Gon Jin Ha Luk*   99
Stir-fried Scallops with Asparagus *Lo Seun Chaau Dai Ji*   100
Scallops in Black Bean Sauce *Si Jap Chaau Dai Ji*   102

Fish & Seafood (continued)

Stir-fried Fresh Crab with Ginger *Geung Chung Chaau Hai*   103
Clams in Black Bean Sauce *Si Jap Chaau Hin*   105
Baby Squid Stuffed with Pork and Mushrooms *Jin Yeung Cheui Tung*   106

Poultry & Meat   108

Bang Bang Chicken *Pang Pang Gai*   116
Chicken in Guilin Chili Bean Paste *Gwai Lam Laat Jeung Gai*   119
Chicken Steamed with Rice in Lotus Leaves *Ho Yip Faan*   120
San Choy Bau *Saang Choi Baau*   122
Chicken with Winter Chestnuts *Leut Ji Man Gai*   123
Chicken with Cashew Nuts *Yiu Gwo Gai Ding*   125
Gong Bao Chicken *Gung Bou Gai*   126
Hainan Chicken Rice *Hoi Maam Gai Faan*   129
Salt-roasted Chicken *Yip Guk Gai*   130
Stir-fried Shredded Chicken with Celery *Kan Choi Chaau Gai Si*   133
Sweet-and-sour Chicken *Gu Lo Gai*   134
Beef Chop Suey *Jaap Seui Ngau Yuk*   137
Braised Beef with Star Anise *Lou Ngau Yuk*   138
Ma Po Doufu *Ma Po Dau Fu*   141
Mongolian Hot Pot *Mung Gu Fo Wo*   144
Stir-fried Beef with Broccoli and Ginger *Laan Fa Chaau Ngau Yuk*   147
Cha Siu *Mat Jap Cha Siu*   148
Lion's Head Casserole *Hung Siu Si Ji Tau*   151
Spareribs in a Sweet-and-sour Sauce *Tong Chou Paai Gwat*   152
Pork Ribs Braised in Soy Sauce *Hung Siu Paai Gwat*   154
Spicy Sichuan Pork *Wui Wo Yuk*   155
Northern Lamb Kabobs *Bak Fong Yeung Yuk Chyun*   156
Xinjiang Lamb Casserole *San Geung Yeung Naam Bou*   157
Xinjiang Rice Pot with Lamb *San Geung Yeung Yuk Faan*   158
Aromatic Duck *Heung Sou Ngaap*   161
Crispy Stuffed Duck *Baat Bou Ngaap*   162
Peking Duck *Bak Ging Tin Ngaap*   165

Rice & Noodles   166

Steamed White Rice *Si Miu Baak Faan*   174
Egg-fried Rice *Daan Fa Chaau Faan*   175
Fried Rice with Pork and Shrimp *Yeung Jau Chaau Faan*   176
Egg Fu Yung *Fu Yung Daan*   177
Ants Climbing a Tree *Maang Ngai Seung Syu*   178
Beef Chow Mein *Ngau Yuk Chaau Min*   181
Chengdu Noodles in Sesame Sauce *Sing Dou Ma Laat Min*   182
Cross the Bridge Noodles *Go Kiu Mai Sin*   185

Rice & Noodles (continued)

Dan Dan Mian *Daam Daam Min*	188
Pork Lo Mein *Yuk Si Lou Min*	191
Rice Noodles with Beef in Black Bean Sauce *Si Jiu Ngau Ho*	192
Singapore Noodles *Sing Jau Chaau Mai*	195

Vegetable Dishes — 196

Braised Straw Mushrooms *Man Dung Gu*	204
Eggplant with Red Bell Peppers *Chou Liu Ke Ji*	207
Sichuan Fried Eggplant *Yu Heung Ke Ji*	208
Stuffed Eggplant with Spicy Sauce *Jin Yeung Ke Ji*	211
Spicy Green Beans *Gon Bin Sei Gai Dau*	212
Stir-fried Long Beans with Red Pepper *Dang Lung Jiu Chaau Dau Go*	214
Stir-fried Bean Sprouts *Ching Chaau Nga Choi*	215
Hot-and-sour Cabbage *Chou Liu Ye Choi*	216
Stir-fried Chinese Greens *Chaau Jaap Choi*	220
Choi Sum in Oyster Sauce *Hou Yau Choi Sam*	221
Broccoli and Snow Pea Stir-fry *Chaau Seung Cheui*	222
Bamboo Shoots with Beancurd *Seun Jim Dau Fu*	225
Scrambled Eggs with Beancurd *Waat Daan Dau Fu*	226
Chunky Potatoes with Cilantro Leaves *Heung Choi Tou Dau*	229
Cabbage and Cucumber in a Vinegar Dressing *Bak Fong Paau Choi*	230
Chinese Tomato Salad *Chung Sik Faan Ke Sa Leut*	231

Desserts — 232

Toffee Apple Slices *Bat Si Ping Gwo*	240
Banana Fritters *Ja Heung Jiu*	243
Mango Pudding *Mong Gwo Bou Din*	244
Fresh Fruit Salad with Lemon Juice *Jaap Gwo Sa Leut*	245
Pears in Honey Syrup *Mat Jin Syut Lei*	246
Winter Rice Pudding with Dried Fruits *Laap Baat Juk*	247
Eight-treasures Sweet Rice Cake *Baat Bou Faan*	248
Almond Jelly in Ginger Sauce *Geung Jap Hang Yan Je Lei*	251
Almond Cookies *Hang Yan Beng*	252

Index — 254

INTRODUCTION

That the Chinese love and are knowledgeable about good food is a statement rarely challenged. This assertion is partly based on the existence of a vast canon of literature about food, both from a technical cooking point of view and from a literary point of view. Artists and intellectuals have traditionally also been gourmets, their knowledge of culinary matters as extensive as their grasp on their own subjects (a fact still largely true today).

Tang dynasty (618-907) poet Tu Fu, a lover of excellence in the culinary as in the literary arts, wrote repeatedly of snow and frost as allusions to the refined techniques of Imperial chefs, brilliantly slivering meat and fish into glittering threads that would all but fly up from the cutting board. Honey was poetically referred to as "sweet dew," a kind of manna from heaven. Confucius was once asked by a king for advice on military matters, to which he replied: "I have indeed heard about matters pertaining to *tsu* (a meat stand) and *tou* (a meat platter) but I have not learned about military matters." It is also true that the most ordinary laborer or cab driver can readily discuss food and show a gourmet's inclination to pursue good foods, particularly during Chinese festivals.

Chefs are highly respected and cooking is considered an art, not a trade for someone who could not find other, better work. Even the apparently humble chopsticks are regarded as a quite brilliant invention, uniquely using the thumb that is otherwise often redundant! It was also Confucius who encouraged the adoption of chopsticks at the table instead of other lethal implements such as knives, and in so doing had a huge influence on the development of the cuisine. If chopsticks are the tools for eating, the food must be cut into a size easily manageable with these eating utensils, or cooked to the correct texture to enable the ready taking apart of larger pieces of meat or vegetables.

The ultimate preoccupation of the Chinese with food can also be understood in terms of the amount of money spent on food. Research has found that as incomes rise in China, so does the percentage of expenditure on food, which goes against global norms. Coupled with this is the amount of time spent preparing dishes and the time spent thinking or talking about food. It is as if the anticipatory discussions on food help dishes taste even better. Elaborate classifications and ritualizations of eating also indicate that food for the Chinese comes, as it were, high up the food chain.

The documentation of Chinese cooking is, as mentioned, almost exhaustive. More than 50 different cooking methods have been minutely identified and defined, including the distinction between open steaming and closed steaming; or between stir-frying, splash-frying, and explode-frying. This is an indication of the close attention paid to the cooking medium or fire control, in addition to the care taken over the quality of ingredients and the flavorings. It has been said

The sun shines down on a roof in the Emperors' former palace, the Forbidden City, in Beijing

that a top chef controls temperature with the same subtleties that a pianist controls the piano's foot pedals. Stir-frying over high heat, perfected by the Cantonese, tends to be perceived abroad as the quintessential Chinese cooking method, though in fact it is a minority technique: in China as a whole, boiling and steaming are actually the most common cooking methods.

Yet the relationship with food among the Chinese can also be seen to be a rather difficult one. Throughout the country's long and complicated dynastic history, and indeed leading into the contemporary Communist Party-led and partial open-market economy period, famine, compounded by periodic flooding, has struck frequently and forcefully. China is the world's third-largest country (after Canada and Russia) and has a population well in excess of one billion. Less than 20 percent of its often rugged landscapes are cultivable. Yet the need to feed so many people is sometimes regarded paradoxically to be at the root of the development of probably the most varied and sophisticated cuisine that exists.

Chinese cooking has at its very foundation the principle of a division between *fan*, the carbohydrates (usually rice or grains, but also noodles, pancakes, or bread), and the *ts'ai*, which essentially represents everything else, from meat, fish and seafood to fresh and preserved vegetables and eggs. The permutations of the *ts'ai* are virtually endless, but the key is to balance the amount of carbohydrate with the meat and vegetable dishes. In times of food shortage or famine, the proportions are, out of necessity, modified, but the concept of the meal never changes.

Left *A street vendor making dumplings*

Overleaf *Towering limestone hills are a feature of China's southern landscape*

The breadth of choice of ingredients is also unmatched. That the Chinese will eat anything is often commented on disdainfully. But this waste-not, want-not ethos, touching everything from learning about wild plants and using every part of the animal—including the blood—to pickling and preserving vegetables when they are plentiful, has given rise to a cuisine with a remarkable diversity in its dishes and cooking methods. Nor has China been shy to adopt fruits, grains, and vegetables introduced by foreigners. Corn and peanuts were introduced by the Portuguese, chilies by the Spanish, and potatoes by the French. Even tomatoes and eggplants are not indigenous. Many such crops became mainstays of the diet when they were found to grow well even in agriculturally poor areas.

Also at the core of Chinese culinary art is the relationship between food and health. Food has always been used as a preventative and curative medicine and almost all Chinese instantly react to illness or the threat of illness through dietary changes. Items most usually seen as medicine, such as ginseng, white fungus, and bird's nests, are also eaten as foods.

At the most basic level, foods are divided into two groups: yin and yang. Yang are heating foods associated with masculinity, while yin are the cooling foods associated with femininity. The classification is more or less common sense: beef, carrots, and chilies are heating; crab, watercress, and cucumber are cooling. The system is important in the composition of a meal, taking into consideration not only what looks good at the market or is in season, but the age and state of health of the diners, and the prevailing weather conditions. Changes in the weather upset the yin–yang balance, hence warming foods such as snake soup or mutton hotchpotch are always eaten as winter approaches. The basic classification is also important for the way in which ingredients are combined in a dish. For example, soybeans (cooling) could be cooked with a little ginger (warming) to balance cool and heat, to make the dish taste good, and also because ginger is a known cure for flatulence.

Essentially, foods from both groups should be eaten in balance. Upsetting that balance is seen as the cause of illness. Cooling foods are used to treat sores, rashes, and fevers, while heating foods treat conditions such as stomach upsets and dry skin. The very specific diet for women after childbirth and during the nursing period includes special soups of fish and chicken. Such beliefs still widely exist today, perhaps because Chinese people love food so much and would rather eat than take medicine!

The equivalent of Christmas or Thanksgiving, with its emphasis on elaborate feasting with family, is Chinese New Year

Lunar New Year

The equivalent of Christmas or Thanksgiving, with its emphasis on elaborate feasting with family, is Chinese New Year, a four-day celebration that falls late in January or early in February. The most important dinner is on the eve of the first day of the festival, when families gather at the home of the grandmother or mother, who is responsible for preparing the dishes.

In ideal circumstances the dinner includes at least eight dishes, eight being a lucky number in Chinese culture, and would almost certainly include delicacies such as abalone and shark's fin. But the expense of the ingredients, and the number of days taken up in their preparation, are not the only considerations.

China is a vast country, dissected by mountain ranges, bordered by cold desert to the north and plateaux to the west, and driven by two major rivers

Each dish is either literally symbolic of good luck, prosperity, and so on, or is given an auspicious name. No dish is ever eaten up entirely, signifying that the family will have more than enough for the year to come.

Steamed chicken is served whole, including head and feet. However, when the chicken is presented, the head is never pointing toward a diner, as superstition says that would bring them bad luck. A fresh fish is very important at the dinner, and the livelier it is before it is killed, the better. This fish is served whole with head and tail intact to symbolize a good beginning and a good ending to the year. Further, to guarantee good fortune, it is essential that the fish is not broken during or after cooking. Stuffed sea cucumber (bêche-de-mer) is a very traditional New Year dish, as is black moss, its long threads representing wealth and prosperity.

Dinner in northern China might not extend to fresh fish and seafood, as this is not always available, but would always include Jiaozi (see page 50) and an Eight-treasures Sweet Rice Cake (see page 248). Noodles are also eaten, their long length symbolizing long life. A superstition says it is bad luck to cut them. A large platter of sweet snack foods precedes the dinner, comprising candied melon (for growth and good health), red melon seeds (red represents joy, happiness, truth, and sincerity), litchi nuts (for good family relationships), kumquats (their golden hue symbolizes prosperity), shredded coconut

Chinese New Year store decorations
welcome in the coming year

(togetherness), dried longans (for many sons), and lotus seeds (for many children). Round, sweet steamed cakes are also shared, their layers symbolizing ever-increasing abundance throughout the year, their round shape signifying the oneness of the family, and the sweetness literally referring to the promise of a rich life.

On the first day of the celebration, many families go to the temple, on the second day a visit is made to the mother's house (the initial dinner is held at the husband's family's home), and the third day is usually spent relaxing at home or shopping. Other highlights include spectacularly noisy lion dances and the receiving of *lai see* or "lucky money."

Toward a definition of Chinese food

China is a vast country, dissected by mountain ranges, bordered by cold desert to the north and plateaux to the west, and driven by two major rivers (the Yangtze River and the Yellow River), which aid the transportation of food items from province to province. While the majority of people are Han Chinese, there also exist huge communities of Tibetans, Mongols, and Uygurs, together with a host of other minorities, often living in the most remote mountainous areas. Buddhism was introduced from India, but soon became incorporated into existing Confucian and Taoist thought. Thus, not only is there no one single language and no one single religion, there is no one single temperament or personality type. The Beijing people are seen as the intellectuals, Shanghai residents as merchants, and the Cantonese as entrepreneurs.

What every region certainly does have in common is the popularity of snack foods sold on the street, though every city or province has its own unique offerings

Is it possible, then, to give a single definition of Chinese food? If it were possible to distill the essence of Chinese cooking, perhaps the only real unifiers would be the ingredients trinity of ginger, scallions, and soy sauce, followed by cabbage, which is eaten all over the country. Still, the ways of preparing cabbage are very different, ranging from pickling and preserving it in the north or eating it finely sliced in marinated salads, to stir-frying seasonal greens at their peak of freshness in the south.

One might also mention rice as a unifier, though in fact rice is traditionally grown and eaten in the southern part of the country, while grains such as wheat and, most traditionally, millet are grown and consumed in the colder north. Rice is, however, becoming more and more popular in the north, as is wheat in the south, though this basic divide does essentially remain.

What every region certainly does have in common is the popularity of snack foods sold on the street, though every city or province has its own unique offerings, from the spicy noodles of Chengdu or the fresh-cut noodles of Beijing to the chicken's feet of Guangzhou and the steamed buns of Shanghai.

Over the centuries, Chinese scholars and gourmets have attempted to define the main regional cuisines in the country according to particular cooking "schools," but perhaps the most simple division is into four general "quarters": the spiciness of the west, the freshness of the east, the delicacy of the south, and the grandeur of the cooking in the north.

Right Street stalls sell fresh snacks throughout the day

The North

The north is the land of long, bitterly cold winters (the freezing winds experienced at the Great Wall can truly take the breath away), bone-dry sandstorms blowing in from the Gobi Desert (which is slowly encroaching on urban centers), and parching hot summers. These factors do not allow for glorious agriculture, though cereals, sweet potato, soybeans, and peanuts can do well. Cabbages and radishes are preserved and stored for those long winter months, and during the summer there is plenty of fresh fruit and vegetables; huge, juicy watermelons are particularly prolific in season.

The dominant cooking of the vast northern tracts, which includes Inner Mongolia, can be referred to as Imperial cuisine. This *haute cuisine* draws from many influences, particularly from the Manchus and Mongolians, as the early emperors were all northerners, preferring meat, and particularly mutton, above all other foods. Later, Shandong cuisine began to make a deep imprint on Imperial dishes, thanks to the travels of its merchants to Beijing. The coastal province of Shandong is famous for its variety of seafood, and for being the birthplace of Confucius, as well as for its inspired use of staple ingredients such as onions.

Imperial dishes are notable for the great care taken in choosing quality ingredients, painstaking preparation, and in the refined tastes achieved. The Imperial kitchens would have employed thousands of staff, and every meal would have been highly elaborate, whether or not there were guests present. While a handful of restaurants in Beijing run by octogenarian chefs claim to keep the spirit of Imperial cooking alive, nothing today could come close to the rampant excesses of the historic Forbidden City.

*A farmer transplants rice seedlings
in a flooded field*

Peking Duck (see page 165) is possibly the most important contribution of the north to the contemporary Chinese culinary repertoire. The specially reared flocks of white-feathered ducks are particularly revered for their skin, which becomes perfectly crispy and barely fatty when cooked. The meat and skin is then served in miniature wheat flour pancakes with slivers of raw scallion and cucumber to cut through any grease, accented with the sweetness of hoisin or plum sauce.

Inner Mongolia has contributed two great dishes to Chinese cooking: the Mongolian grill and Mongolian hotchpotch. These dishes provide immediate warmth for diners as well as a highly social cooking medium, both no doubt created as excellent recipes for long winter nights.

The nomadic herdsmen of the north were often Muslim and their foods quickly spread across the northern frontiers and to Beijing. The diet would not allow for pork, of course, and the preferred meat has always been mutton, as it remains.

Shandong Province is particularly famous today for its beer production based around Qingdao, and also for its viticulture. A government directive some years back spawned an active wine market, although Chinese wine is still comparatively expensive. Perhaps the best wines, so far, are being produced in nearby Shanxi Province, which may also be where grape cultivation first began. However, this once politically important province, where many rebellions were launched (the movie *Raise the Red Lantern* was filmed in one of its beautifully preserved compounds), is better known for the excellence of its dark vinegars, potatoes, tomatoes, and wheat noodles.

The South

The food of the south of China, often referred to generally as Cantonese, is regarded as the height

The Cantonese are famed for their dim sum, *little snack foods eaten with tea in a meal known as* yum cha *(literally "to drink tea")*

of Chinese cuisine, and not only by the Cantonese themselves, who regard it as the most sophisticated in the world. In the north, there is a riddle about what the Cantonese will eat: that if it has legs but is not a table, and has wings but is not a plane, then it counts as food. In addition to using every part of every animal or fish, the Cantonese adore experimenting with different ingredients, and the variety of the cuisine is extraordinary.

The intricate balance of flavors, textures, and colors is one of the most important elements of its excellence, while the careful cutting of ingredients and the art of stir-frying, which cooks each slivered item rapidly while retaining texture, are the tools.

The insistence on, and availability of, a vast and varied selection of fresh and high-quality produce is another element in the Cantonese claim to excellence. The subtropical climate means a long growing season, and there is some very fertile land. Fresh vegetables, typically bell peppers, eggplants, onions, tomatoes, and many kinds of greens, are available all year round. Bananas, litchis, and papayas are among the best of the seasonal fruits available, and China's highest quality rice comes from the vast flooded paddies of southern Guangzhou.

This region is bordered by sea, yet also produces much freshwater produce in its rivers and fish farms. Pig and chicken farming are big business. Chickens are almost always killed upon purchase, while pigs are slaughtered and butchered just hours before arriving at market.

The Cantonese are famed for their *dim sum*, little snack foods eaten with tea in a meal known as *yum cha* (literally "to drink tea"). Dim sum encompasses a vast selection of tiny steamed items ranging from the famous shrimp-stuffed *har gau* and pork-stuffed *siu mai* to delicious sweet steamed buns, chicken's feet, and small bowls of congee. The dim sum kitchen is highly regarded among the Cantonese and the art of wrapping, rolling, chopping, and steaming can take a lifetime of learning.

Within Cantonese cooking are three distinct cooking traditions, which are attributed to the Chiu Chow, Hainanese, and the Hakka peoples. Chiu Chow cooking tends to be overshadowed by the others, but is still highly regarded. The hot or cold goose dishes, including liver and blood, soups, and fish balls, are among its best offerings. Subtropical Hainan Island is a favored vacation destination for mainland Chinese, but some of its indigenous cooking survives, particularly in the form of the well-known Hainan Chicken Rice (see page 129). The food of the Hakka people is at best simple, but cooked with beautiful balance. Fresh vegetables retain their crispness through judicious cooking, particularly in the absence of any heavy oils or flavorings such as garlic. Salt-baked chicken and vegetables, such as bitter melon or long chilies coated with fish paste and fried, are two specialties.

Cantonese food is the Chinese regional cuisine best known to the outside world, although this knowledge is less of a reflection on the quality of the cuisine and more about the emigration patterns from this region to the West in the nineteenth and twentieth centuries. Migrants opened take-out diners and restaurants as businesses, and thus Cantonese cooking became synonymous with Chinese cooking. If one restaurant was successful, a newcomer would simply duplicate the menu. Hence the easy familiarity of dishes with names such as chop suey, sweet-and-sour, chow mein, and so on, which may or may not have their roots in the kitchens of Guangdong. The majority of Cantonese living in China would regard the cooking in many so-called Cantonese restaurants with surprise.

The East

Shanghai was once one of the world's great cities, and is destined to return to that status again as China's economic boom, and Shanghai's favorable position and local culture, thrust it ahead of the rest of the country. The city boasts an illustrious, internationally orientated history and because of this, is at the center of the cooking of the eastern region, which stretches along the eastern coast through Jiangsu and Zheijiang. Trading at the port of Shanghai created great wealth, and along with it knowledge and exposure. The foreign concessions of the British, French, and Russians brought their own culinary influences to bear, and all kinds of breads, cakes, and pastries were introduced.

Shanghai's proximity to sea, and huge lakes and rivers, complemented by rich agricultural lands, created a gourmet's paradise. It is known as "the land of fish and rice," and indeed the seasonal freshwater hairy crab of Shanghai remains a sought-after and very expensive treat. Eel is another delicacy from here. The region is also particularly famous for its vinegars and rice wine. Chinkiang black vinegar, akin to Italian balsamic vinegar, and Shaoxing rice wine are among the top examples in China.

The cooking associated with Shanghai typically incorporates generous amounts of oil, rock sugar, rice wine, and vinegar. Sometimes it might seem a little oily or a little too sweet, but it can do wonders with the simplest ingredients and at its best it is a beautifully balanced cuisine.

In Hong Kong, partly because apartments are usually too tiny but for the smallest family gatherings, the majority of eating, especially social eating, is done outside the home

Almost as famous as the cooking of Shanghai is the unique cuisine of Fujian, the province lying south of Zheijiang. This province directly faces Taiwan, and their cooking styles continue to influence each other. Fujian chefs are most famous for their soups (even more famous than the Cantonese), which range from the thinnest broths to something more akin to a stew. Such stews, whether of meat or vegetable, are mostly started with shortening, then slow-simmered until extremely soft.

The West

The far west corner of China (including the vast province of Tibet) borders Nepal, India, Bhutan, Myanmar, Laos and Vietnam. It was through these routes that Buddhism, originally from India, arrived in China, and Muslim influences also remain strong. Certainly, it could be argued that the most spicy cuisine of China was influenced by the cuisines of a number of these neighbors, and there are shared foods and cooking styles.

The region is also one of great beauty with huge mountain passes, vast forests, beautiful lakes and rivers, and Kunming, the capital of Yunnan Province, is famous for its varied plant life. At the same time, some parts of this region remain quite inaccessible and consequently poor.

The culinary heart of the region is Sichuan Province and its capital, Chengdu. There is a saying that, in rough translation from the Chinese, runs along the line of, "China is the place for food, but Sichuan is the place for flavor."

And Sichuan cooking does have flavor! Chilies were introduced into China by the Jesuits, and were soon embraced in the Chinese kitchen. Chilies now feature prominently, either pickled or dried.

The Sichuan pepper, a tiny pink flower-shaped spice, brings a unique aroma, and tongue-numbing effect, to the region's cooking. There's a Chinese joke that suggests the people of Sichuan eat this tongue-numbing pepper in order to be able to enjoy an even greater number of chilies! Chilies are one of the best sources of vitamins C and A in the vegetable world, and are also believed to be perfect for the less-than-perfect Sichuan climate. Heavy, humid skies create a wet gray blanket for most of the year, slowing down the body. Chilies help the body to excrete water, whether during cold humid winters or hot humid summers.

Various bean pastes, sesame pastes, and preserved vegetables also contribute to the striking flavor profiles of Sichuan cooking. It should not be overlooked, however, that like other cuisines known for the heat of their dishes, there is a complementary repertoire of dishes that soothe, cleanse, and balance the palate, creating balance during the meal.

Sichuan cooking has yet to gain a firm Western following, but is revered within China, at least among those who can handle the chilies. Classics from the region such as Ma Po Doufu (see page 141), Gong Bao Chicken (see page 126), and Dan Dan Mian (see page 188) are becoming increasingly popular, and by necessity often offered in non-Sichuanese restaurants. Camphor and tea-smoked ducks are also a classic of the region. Yunnan Province, on the border with Vietnam, Laos, and Myanmar, produces the most famous cured hams of China. There are moves afoot in China to begin to classify top-quality produce in the French manner, in much the same way as Champagne can only be made in Champagne and Bresse chicken has to be born and bred in Bresse. This ham, with its strong and very meaty flavor, is usually braised or added to soups, and it follows that pork here is of excellent quality and that lard is the usual cooking medium. The high-quality pu-erh tea is also from Yunnan. These items apart, this region's cuisine, heavily featuring yogurt, fried milk curd, and cheese, is mostly hidden from the world.

The Chinese restaurant

The Chinese restaurant is a great institution. In Hong Kong, partly because apartments are usually too tiny but for the smallest family gatherings, the majority of eating, especially social eating, is done outside the home. Corporate entertaining in restaurants is a very significant part of any relationship or business deal.

It is important to understand that restaurant cooking often reaches heights that are impossible in the domestic kitchen. This is partly to do with the hardware, as restaurant or hotel kitchens have space for massive wok sections fired with fierce flames. Deep-fryers and ovens are similarly too large to have at home. The skills of the trained chef, practicing and perfecting his art every day, cannot be matched by the amateur either. Access to the best ingredients, highly developed cutting and cooking techniques, and an instinct for split-second timing all give restaurant food the potential to make the labors of the home cook look rather humble.

A man serves up a bowl of hot noodles for a quick between-meal snack

In metropolitan centers like Beijing, Shenzen, and Shanghai, it is easy to experience good food, particularly street food

These are some of the reasons for the burgeoning restaurant scene in Hong Kong, unmatched by any other Chinese city. In the West, a Chinese restaurant might serve over 100 dishes, principally Cantonese but with a few northern dishes thrown in, but some restaurants in Hong Kong are specialized and serve only one dish, perhaps won ton noodle soup, congee, or hotchpotch, or just one kind of product such as dim sum, fish, or pigeon. Regional restaurants abound too, whether Chiu Chow, Sichuan, or Shanghainese, reflecting the movements of the early immigrants from mainland China into the city state.

Restaurant culture is now reviving in many other parts of China, though there remains too often a division between tourist and local restaurants. It goes without saying that the local restaurants are better, though it is also true that in smaller towns, the typical food may not be of high quality and may not be to the taste of the typical foreign traveler. In metropolitan centers like Beijing, Shenzen and Shanghai, it is easy to experience good food, particularly street food such as noodles, jiaozi dumplings, and buns.

The typical Chinese restaurant, and this is true of Chinese restaurants anywhere in the world, is cavernous, noisy, apparently a little chaotic, and very

The Imperial Vault of Heaven in Beijing, seen through an impressive entrance gate

often a bit dusty around the edges. This may reflect the restaurant movement after 1949, when attempts to reduce the elitist nature of cooking led to large spaces that could be shared by many people. But space for large tables suits the typically multi-generational family group, and in the case of dim sum restaurants, where piles of bamboo baskets are traditionally wheeled around the restaurant and offered to all tables, this system allows for the food always to be served piping hot.

There is, then, little etiquette in Chinese restaurants, where the most important element is always the quality (and amount) of food. Food and tea can be spilt on the tablecloth (if there is one), but no one will worry and certainly the waiter won't rush over to clear the mess. Diners usually serve themselves from the communal dishes, and choosing the pieces of meat or fish closest to you is regarded as good manners. Serving a guest or a neighbor with food is also widely practiced and the host is very likely to extract the best part of the fish and present it to an honored guest. Pouring tea for others, before you pour for yourself, is de rigueur. Chopstick etiquette is also important: when not in use, they should be laid on their rest or on a plate, never stuck into the bowl. Pointing with chopsticks is considered rather rude.

Whether or not to finish your own bowl of rice, whether to finish all the food in the communal dishes, and whether to refuse a dish are all matters of change and debate. Past generations often have a tendency to finish everything, with memories of war-rationing and even famine, and the Chinese are no different here. The younger generations may have a different approach. But in general, these protocols should not be worried about too much. Every nationality encourages other nationalities to try their food, and will show delight if their food is enjoyed and well received.

In the Chinese kitchen

Incredibly, most southern Chinese families have little more than two gas rings, a rice cooker, a tiny shelf-top oven, and these days, perhaps a microwave. Farther north, the kitchen might be as simple as a bench with holes in it for woks or pans, fired from below with charcoal or coal. The essential cooking implements of the Chinese kitchen are:

Cutting board Thick, wooden boards are traditionally used, as wood is much better for preserving the quality of knives than other materials and doesn't harbor germs.

Chopsticks In addition to chopsticks (and rests) for table use, most cooks would use a large wooden pair for tossing and stirring foods in the wok.

Clay pot This is the traditional, inexpensive pot with a glazed inside. These are excellent for braising and also for making soup.

Cleaver The cleaver does everything from chopping vegetables and slicing meat through the bone to carrying ingredients to the pot and even bashing (with the handle end).

Spatula A pair of large wooden spatulas is ideal for stir-frying in the wok, particularly when noodles are involved.

Steamer The Chinese traditionally use bamboo baskets in various sizes, balanced in the wok, but a Western steamer works just as well.

Wok The best are made of cast-iron. Woks should be washed with detergent as little as possible, but rather wiped out with water. This technique creates what is known as "wok taste" which, it has been suggested, might even include a little iron. The wok should be preheated before adding oil to get the oil really hot.

In the Chinese pantry

Bamboo shoots Fresh bamboo shoots, if available, should be peeled and boiled in water for 30 minutes before use. Rinse the canned version before use.

Beancurd Made from soybeans, beancurd is highly nutritious. It has almost no flavor, but absorbs flavors beautifully. The two main kinds are soft (for soups and stir-frying) and firm (for deep-frying and braising). Store covered in water before use.

Bean sprouts There are two main kinds—soybean sprouts (oval yellow heads) and mung bean sprouts (round green heads). Store in a covering of water, changed daily.

Cha siu A honey-glazed pork preparation used to add flavor to other dishes (see page 148).

Chili bean sauce As the name suggests, this sauce is principally made with chilies and beans, either soybeans or black beans. Some sauces need to be cooked, others, such as Guilin chili bean paste, can also be used straight from the jar as a spread or dip.

Chili oil This can be made at home by pouring smoking oil over a pile of chili flakes, but can also be purchased in small bottles.

Conpoy Dried scallops have a very strong flavor and aroma and should be soaked in boiling water before use, then shredded and used in soups and stuffings.

Cilantro The leaves are frequently used as a garnish, though the Chinese do not use the roots.

Dipping sauces The Chinese use a number of dipping sauces, usually based on soy sauce or vinegar, with specific dishes. These can easily be made at home or often bought in Asian food stores.

Jiaozi Dipping Sauce Stir together 1 tablespoon each of soy sauce and vinegar, 1/2 teaspoon of sugar, and 1 teaspoon each of chopped ginger and garlic.

Sesame and Scallion Dipping Sauce
Combine 2 tablespoons of light soy sauce, 1/4 teaspoon of sesame oil, and 2 teaspoons of finely chopped scallion and pour into small individual dishes.

Soy Mustard Dipping Sauce Whisk together 3 tablespoons of light soy sauce, 1 1/2 tablespoons of mustard powder, 2 tablespoons of chicken stock, 1/2 teaspoon of salt, and 1 teaspoon of sesame oil until well combined.

Dried mushrooms The most commonly dried mushroom is in the same family as the shiitake. They are available in a number of price brackets, the thicker versions being the most expensive. Soak in warm water before use.

Dried shrimp Soak in warm water or rice wine before use. They impart a strong flavor to stuffings, soups, and fried rice.

Fermented black beans With their excellent flavor, these bring a color contrast to any dish and can be used whole or mashed. Always wash them before use.

Ginger A vital ingredient in Chinese cooking for flavor and aroma. Use as fresh as possible. It also helps to disguise any unpleasant cooking smells.

Laap cheung Southern Chinese preserved pork sausage with a slightly sweet flavor. Use finely sliced or minced.

yuk Chinese preserved bacon.

Noodles Rice noodles are made from ground rice and come in two forms: flat ones (also known as rice sticks), which can be fresh or dried, and very thin rice vermicelli. Egg noodles are available in all shapes and sizes, either fresh or dried. They are usually sold in little mounds. Beanthread noodles are very fine semitransparent noodles made from mung bean starch. They are used in noodle dishes and also in hotchpotches.

Oyster sauce A highly flavored sauce that is very popular in Cantonese cooking. It is added at the last minute to accent vegetables, meat, and fish.

Pancakes

Peking duck pancakes can usually be found in Asian stores, but are simple to make at home. They can be reheated in a steamer or microwave oven.

To make 30 pancakes, sift 3 cups flour and a pinch of salt into a bowl and slowly stir in 1 1/4 cups boiling water to make a thick dough. Add 2 tablespoons of cold water and 1/2 teaspoon of sesame oil, then knead the dough for 4 minutes until it is soft and smooth. Cover and rest for 30 minutes. Dust a counter with flour, then divide the dough into 2 and knead until smooth. Roll each portion into a log and divide into 15 balls. Roll each out to create a 6-inch/15-cm circle. Heat a dry skillet, then turn down the heat. Place the pancakes in the skillet and cook until little brown spots begin to appear. Flip and cook for an additional 10 seconds.

Pepper Ground white pepper is the pepper most often used in Chinese cooking.

Plum sauce Excellent as a dipping sauce for spring rolls or with duck.

Preserved vegetables Made from mustard cabbage, this is sometimes called Sichuan pickle. There is also preserved turnip which has a sour, slightly spicy taste.

Rice White rice is more popular than brown or red rice, though the latter two are usually cheaper and are more nutritious. Glutinous rice, which should be soaked for a few hours in water before steaming, is more often used for desserts.

Rice vinegar Rice vinegar can be white (more subtle) or quite dark and is made from a mix of glutinous rice and grains. Look for the Chinkiang vinegar, which is almost like a balsamic vinegar.

Rock sugar Transparent blocks of sugar with a pleasant aroma.

Sesame oil Made with roasted sesame seeds, this is an excellent flavoring for many dishes, but use sparingly as it is very strong. This oil is rarely cooked, but should be added just before the dish is served or incorporated into cold dishes.

Sesame paste Strong in flavor and thick in texture, this should be mixed with chicken stock or water before use to create a good consistency.

Shaoxing rice wine The wine of Shaoxing in eastern Zheijiang Province is the best quality rice wine and a vital ingredient in Chinese cooking. This yellow rice wine is used in marinades and for braising. Sherry is a possible substitute, but is quite different in flavor.

Sichuan peppers The pink mouth-numbing spice so distinctive of Sichuan cooking. Known as *hua jiao* in Chinese.

Soy sauce A quintessential flavoring in Chinese cooking, made from fermented soybeans. Light soy sauce is the thinner, saltier version, used as a seasoning. Dark soy sauce is heavier and richer, used in braising and in marinades, particularly to give color.

Scallions Vital in Chinese cooking for color, taste, and aroma.

Star anise An attractive and highly aromatic spice: excellent in stews.

Stock The Chinese usually grade stocks as "everyday" and "superior" and they are a vital foundation for Chinese cooking. This recipe is for a simple everyday chicken stock. To upgrade it, add pork ribs and sections of duck, including the skin and bones.

Bring a pan of water to s boil and plunge a whole chicken or chicken pieces, including the skin and bones, into it. Remove after 1 minute. Put the chicken, 2 celery stalks, a piece of peeled ginger, 2 scallions, and 1 bay leaf into a large pan with generous 2^1/$_2$ quarts of water and bring to a boil. Cover and simmer for 1^1/$_2$ to 2 hours, skimming the surface frequently.

Tangerine peel This can be made at home simply by placing the skin of a mandarin orange in a very dry place, or it can be purchased from Asian food stores.

Skins The Chinese use both soft and hard wheat skins to enclose their spring rolls, won tons, and dumplings. Soft spring roll skins can be made at home, or skins can be found refrigerated in Asian food stores and frozen until needed.

To make 20 soft spring roll skins, sift 3 cups all-purpose flour into a bowl with 1 teaspoon of salt. Make a well in the center and stir in 4 beaten eggs. Slowly add 1^3/$_4$ cups cold water, whisking to create a smooth and thick batter. Finally stir in 6 tablespoons of vegetable oil. To cook the skins, heat a small 6-inch/15-cm nonstick skillet, then drop a scant ^{1}/$_4$ cup of the batter into the skillet and swirl. Let cook until the edges peel away from the skillet. Pile the skins on top of each other, then bring to the table for wrapping.

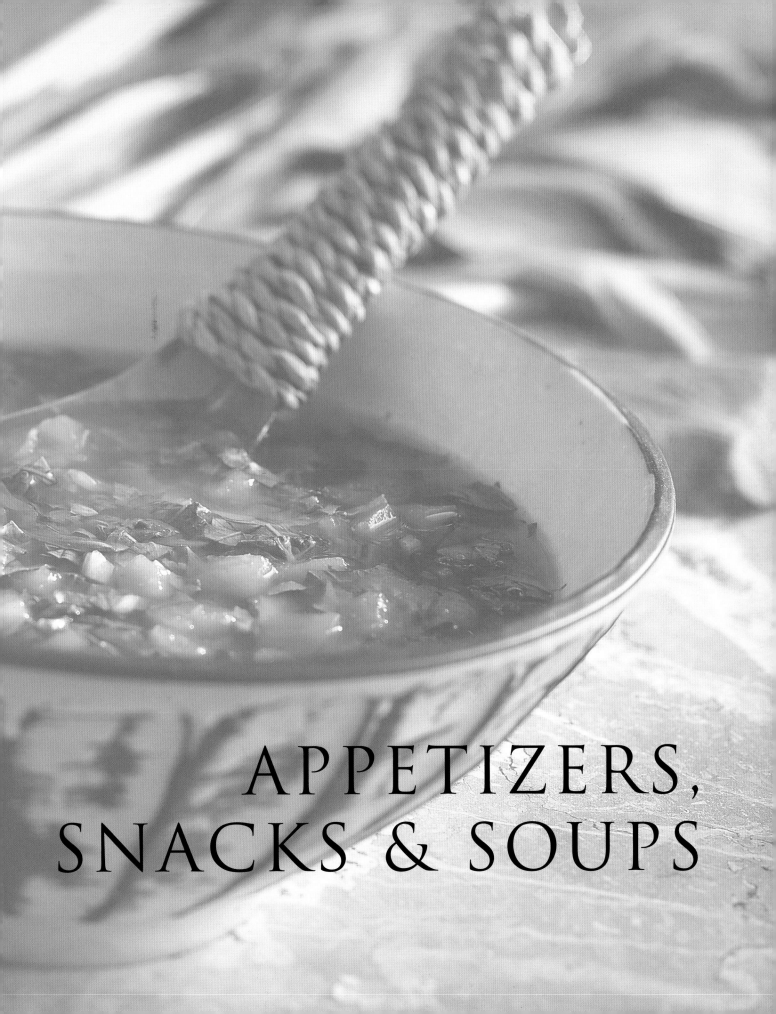

APPETIZERS, SNACKS & SOUPS

Chinese meals are structured in a quite different manner from the Western concept of courses. Thus a soup might be eaten throughout the meal or at the end of it, rather than at the beginning, or maybe even for breakfast such as the Congee with Fish Fillet (see page 62). Appetizers may not arrive before the entrées, and snacks, as the name implies, could be eaten any time, anywhere, such as in the middle of a shopping trip or while sightseeing.

No tourist destination in China would be without a collection of little food stalls at the entrance, selling all kinds of onion cakes, noodles, dumplings, steamed buns, and fresh fruit or nuts. The Chinese are great snackers, although these days some of those snacks are as likely to come from packages as to be bought freshly made on the street.

However, there is a strong tradition throughout China of teasing the appetite before a meal by sharing a selection of small, cold dishes, which might include cold meats, such as sliced goose with soy sauce, jellyfish, a fish dish, like Whitebait with Green Chili (see page 57), pickled vegetables, or a marinated vegetable, such as Marinated Soybeans (see page 60). These might well be on the table before diners sit down or, in a restaurant setting, represent the Chinese equivalent of *amuse bouches* in French culinary culture.

Soups, which are almost exclusively clear soups, are particularly important in Chinese cuisine. Soups are used as a tonic, as preventative medicine, and to help protect the body from extremes of weather. Dishes such as shark's fin soup or snake soup are expensive, prestigious, gourmet delicacies, served at banquets or on other important occasions. A basic

Right A shop-keeper weighs her customer's goods

chicken stock is vital to the Chinese kitchen, often forming the base for the daily soup. Simply simmering a few different ingredients in a base stock can transform the flavor and appearance into something quite new. Sometimes such soups, with many different meats and vegetables added, resemble meals in their own right, but they are almost always light, even such an impressive soup as Whole Chicken Soup (see page 71). Soups, such as the delicate Sichuan Pumpkin Soup (see page 67), also serve to freshen or cleanse the palate after a series of spicy Sichuan dishes. Thus there are no rules as to exactly when during the meal the soups should be served. While high-class Chinese restaurants might serve diners separately, elsewhere a huge tureen is almost always brought to the table, and diners simply serve themselves and others. Soups are normally drunk, rather than eaten with a spoon.

One of the most important snack foods in China is Cantonese dim sum, an array of dozens of dishes including steamed and fried dumplings and buns,

The skilled dim sum chef is revered as an artist, and few people would ever attempt to prepare dim sum in their own kitchens

savory or sweet, small bowls of noodles or congee, and items such as chicken's feet. This popular snack or meal can be eaten at any time from breakfast to lunch, together with tea. The skilled dim sum chef is revered as an artist, and few people would ever attempt to prepare dim sum in their own kitchens. The great southern weekend tradition of *yum cha* (literally "to drink tea," but including the eating of dim sum) is a highly social occasion for family and friends outside the home.

Overleaf *The Imperial Forbidden City in Beijing dominates the city's skyline*

spring rolls
cheun gyun

MAKES 20–25 PIECES

6 dried Chinese mushrooms, soaked in
warm water for 20 minutes

1 tbsp vegetable or peanut oil

2 cups ground pork

1 tsp dark soy sauce

1 cup fresh or canned bamboo shoots,
rinsed and julienned (if using fresh shoots,
boil in water first for 30 minutes)

pinch of salt

3^1/$_2$ oz/100 g raw shrimp, peeled, deveined, and
chopped

generous 1^1/$_2$ cups bean sprouts, trimmed and coarsely
chopped

1 tbsp finely chopped scallions

25 spring roll skins*

1 egg white, lightly beaten

vegetable or peanut oil, for deep-frying

1 Squeeze out any excess water from the mushrooms and finely slice, discarding any tough stems.

2 In a preheated wok or deep pan, heat the tablespoon of oil and stir-fry the pork until it changes color. Add the dark soy sauce, bamboo shoots, mushrooms, and a little salt. Stir over high heat for 3 minutes.

3 Add the shrimp and cook for 2 minutes, then add the beansprouts and cook for an additional minute. Remove from the heat and stir in the scallion. Let cool.

4 Place a tablespoon of the mixture toward the bottom of a skin. Roll once to secure the filling, then fold in the sides to create a 4-inch/10-cm piece and continue to roll up. Seal with egg white.

5 Heat enough oil for deep-frying in a wok, deep-fat fryer or large heavy-bottom pan until it reaches 180–190°C/350–375°F, or until a cube of bread browns in 30 seconds. Without overcrowding the pan, fry the rolls for about 5 minutes until golden brown and crispy.

*cook's tip
Fresh, wheat-based spring roll skins are the best, about 9 inches/23 cm in diameter, but smaller versions can be used to make smaller rolls. Frozen versions are also acceptable, or use lumpia skins from the Philippines.

vegetarian spring rolls
sou choi cheun gyun

1 Squeeze out any excess water from the mushrooms and finely chop, discarding any tough stems. Drain the beanthread noodles and coarsely chop.

2 In a preheated wok or deep pan, heat the oil, then toss in the ginger and cook until fragrant. Add the mushrooms and stir for about 2 minutes. Add the carrot, cabbage, and scallion and stir-fry for 1 minute. Add the beanthread noodles and light soy sauce and stir-fry for 1 minute. Add the beancurd and cook for an additional minute. Season with the salt, pepper, and sugar and mix well. Continue cooking for 1–2 minutes, or until the carrot is soft. Remove from the heat and let the mixture cool.

3 Place a scant tablespoon of the mixture toward the bottom of a skin. Roll once to secure the filling, then fold in the sides to create a 4-inch/10-cm piece and continue to roll up. Seal with egg white.

4 Heat enough oil for deep-frying in a wok, deep-fat fryer, or large heavy-bottom pan until it reaches 350–375°F/180–190°C, or until a cube of bread browns in 30 seconds. Without overcrowding the pan, cook the rolls for about 5 minutes, or until golden brown and crispy. Serve with a good soy sauce for dipping.

*cook's tip
It is less authentic, but delicious small-size rolls can be made with rice-paper skins, brushed with hot water to soften them. These are also easier to handle than wheat skins.

MAKES 18–20 PIECES

6 dried Chinese mushrooms, soaked in
  warm water for 20 minutes
2 oz/55 g beanthread noodles, soaked in
  warm water for 20 minutes
2 tbsp vegetable or peanut oil
1 tbsp finely chopped fresh gingerroot
generous 2/3 cup carrot, julienned
scant 1 cup finely shredded cabbage
1 tbsp finely sliced scallion
1 tbsp light soy sauce
3 oz/85 g soft beancurd, cut into small cubes
1/2 tsp salt
pinch of white pepper
pinch of sugar
20 spring roll skins*
1 egg white, lightly beaten
vegetable or peanut oil, for deep-frying

soft-wrapped pork and shrimp rolls
chung sik yut naam cheun gyun

MAKES 20 PIECES

4 oz/115 g firm beancurd*

3 tbsp vegetable or peanut oil

1 tsp finely chopped garlic

2 oz/55 g lean pork, shredded

4 oz/115 g raw shrimp, peeled and deveined

1/2 small carrot, cut into short thin sticks

1/2 cup fresh or canned bamboo shoots,
    rinsed and shredded (if using fresh shoots,
    boil in water first for 30 minutes)

1 cup very finely sliced cabbage

1/2 cup snow peas, julienned

1–egg omelet, shredded

1 tsp salt

1 tsp light soy sauce

1 tsp Shaoxing rice wine

pinch of white pepper

20 Soft Spring Roll Skins (see page 31)

chili bean sauce, to serve

These rolls can be prepared in the kitchen, though it is far nicer for each diner to roll his or her own at the table, adjusting the amount of chili bean sauce to taste.

1 Slice the beancurd into thin slices horizontally and cook in 1 tablespoon of the oil until it turns golden brown. Cut into thin strips and set aside.

2 In a preheated wok or deep pan, heat the remaining oil and stir-fry the garlic until fragrant. Add the pork and stir for about 1 minute, then add the shrimp and stir for an additional minute. One by one, stirring well after each, add the carrot, bamboo shoots, cabbage, snow peas, beancurd, and, finally, the shredded omelet. Season with the salt, light soy sauce, Shaoxing rice wine, and pepper. Stir for an additional minute, then turn into a serving dish.

3 To assemble each roll, smear a skin with a little chili bean sauce and place a heaped teaspoon of the filling toward the bottom of the circle. Roll up the bottom edge to secure the filling, turn in the sides, and continue to roll up gently.

cook's tip
Chill the firm beancurd to make it easier to handle.

shrimp toasts
ha do si

This delicious Cantonese snack is a great party food.

MAKES 16 PIECES

3¹/₂ oz/100g raw shrimp, peeled, and deveined

2 egg whites

2 tbsp cornstarch

¹/₂ tsp sugar

pinch of salt

2 tbsp finely chopped cilantro leaves

2 slices day-old white bread

vegetable or peanut oil, for deep-frying

1 Pound the shrimp to a pulp in a pestle and mortar or with the base of a cleaver.

2 Mix the shrimp with one of the egg whites and 1 tablespoon of the cornstarch. Add the sugar and salt and stir in the cilantro. Mix the remaining egg white with the remaining cornstarch.

3 Remove the crusts from the bread and cut each slice into 8 triangles. Brush the top of each piece with the egg white and cornstarch mixture, then add 1 teaspoon of the shrimp mixture. Smooth the top.

4 Heat enough oil for deep-frying in a wok, deep-fat fryer, or large heavy-bottom pan until it reaches 350–375°F/180–190°C, or until a cube of bread browns in 30 seconds. Without overcrowding the wok, cook the toasts shrimp-side up for about 2 minutes. Turn and cook for an additional 2 minutes, or until beginning to turn golden brown. Drain and serve warm.

scallion cakes
chung yau beng

*A delicious snack sold piping hot on the streets
in northern China.*

MAKES 12 PIECES

3 cups all-purpose flour

1 tsp salt

1¹⁄₄ cups boiling water

1 tbsp cold water

¹⁄₄ cup shortening

5 oz/140 g scallions, coarsely chopped

1 tsp sea salt

vegetable or peanut oil, for frying

1 Sift the flour and salt into a bowl, then stir in the boiling water and mix thoroughly. Add the cold water and when cool enough, knead the dough on a board until thick and smooth. Place in a bowl, then cover with a damp cloth and set aside for at least 20 minutes.

2 On a lightly floured board, knead the dough for a couple of minutes and divide into 12 pieces. With a lightly floured rolling pin, roll out each piece until thin. Smear with shortening, then dot with scallion and sprinkle with the salt. Re-form into a ball and roll out again into a 4-inch/10-cm diameter circle.

3 In a nonstick skillet, heat 1 teaspoon of the oil, then cook one pancake at a time for 3 minutes each side, gently squashing it into the oil to insure a smooth surface and shaking the pan from time to time. Serve immediately.

onion pancakes
heung chung bok beng

There are dozens of variations on the scallion cake, coming in all textures and sizes. This one is soft and melting, very similar to the crêpes traditionally eaten at Lent in the West.

MAKES ABOUT 16 PIECES

4 tbsp oil

4 tbsp finely sliced scallion

2 eggs

2 egg yolks

1¹/3 cups all-purpose flour

1 tsp salt

1³/4 cups milk

generous ³/4 cup water

1 Heat 1 tablespoon of the oil in a skillet and lightly cook the scallion until beginning to soften. Remove and set aside.

2 Lightly beat the eggs together with the egg yolks and set aside. Sift the flour and salt into a large bowl and lightly mix in the eggs.

3 Slowly add the milk and water, beating by hand, until the batter is creamy. Stir in the remaining oil and continue to beat for a few more minutes. Finally, stir in the scallion.

4 In a nonstick skillet, pour in 1 tablespoon of the batter and cook until set but not brown. To serve, loosely roll the pancakes and cut each one into 3 pieces*.

*cook's tip
Although these pancakes can be eaten as a snack or together with other dishes, they also make great little skins for crispy meat or crunchy vegetables.

A detail from the windows of the teahouse at Yu Yuan Gardens in Shanghai

jiaozi
gaau ji

These crescent-shaped dumplings are extremely popular in central and northern China and bear a time-honored history, moving from the status of a common snack to a specialty dish associated with festivals. They originated from won tons.

MAKES ABOUT 50 PIECES

4 cups ground pork, not too lean

1 tbsp light soy sauce

1¹/₂ tsp salt

1 tsp Shaoxing rice wine

¹/₂ tsp sesame oil

scant 1 cup very finely chopped cabbage

2 tsp minced fresh gingerroot

2 tsp finely chopped scallion

¹/₂ tsp white pepper

50 round won ton skins, about
   2³/₄ inches/7 cm in diameter

Jiaozi Dipping Sauce (see page 29)

1 For the filling, mix the pork with the light soy sauce and ¹/₂ teaspoon salt. Stir carefully, always in the same direction, to create a thick paste. Add the Shaoxing and sesame oil and continue mixing in the same direction. Cover and let rest for at least 20 minutes.

2 To prepare the cabbage, sprinkle the fine shreds with the remaining salt to help draw out the water. Add the ginger, scallion, and white pepper and knead for at least 5 minutes into a thick paste. Combine with the filling.

3 To make the dumplings, place about 1 tablespoon of the filling in the center of each skin, holding the skin in the palm of one hand. Moisten the edges with water, then seal the edges with 2 or 3 pleats on each side and place on a lightly floured board.

4 To cook the dumplings, bring 4 cups water to a rolling boil in a large pan or stockpot. Drop in about 20 dumplings at a time, stirring gently with a chopstick to prevent them sticking together. Cover, then bring back to a boil and cook for 2 minutes. Uncover and add about 7 fl oz/200 ml cold water. Bring back to a boil, cover and cook for an additional 2 minutes.

5 Pour the dipping sauce into individual bowls, then dip the jiaozi in the sauce and eat*.

*cook's tip

Preparation time for this recipe is long, hence huge quantities are usually made at one time. Proportions shown here are an attempt to keep the wrapping time manageable! The dough can be made at home, but it is far easier, of course, to buy the skins. Any remaining cooked dumplings can be fried later to become what are colloquially known as "potstickers."

dumplings in a cold spicy sauce
choi yuk wun tun

The sauce looks spicy and oily, but in fact provides a perfect backdrop for these easy-to-prepare won ton dumplings.

MAKES 20 PIECES

for the dumplings

1 tsp vegetable or peanut oil

1³/4 cups ground pork, not too lean

1 tsp salt

¹/2 tsp white pepper

20 square wheat skins

for the sauce

scant ¹/2 cup vegetable or peanut oil

1 tbsp dried chili flakes

1 tsp sesame oil

1 tsp sugar

1 tbsp light soy sauce

¹/2 tsp white pepper

1 tsp salt

1 garlic clove, finely chopped

1 To prepare the filling, heat the oil in a small pan and stir-fry the pork with the salt and pepper for 3-4 minutes, stirring to break up any meat clumps and letting the juices begin to come out.

2 To prepare the sauce, heat the oil until smoking in a wok or deep pan and pour over the chili flakes. Let cool, then stir in all the other ingredients.

3 To make the dumplings, hold a skin in the palm of one hand and place a scant teaspoon of the filling in the center. Wet the edges and fold over to create a triangle then, with the point facing toward you at the bottom of your index finger, cross the edges behind your finger, sealing with a little water. Take the point facing toward you and turn up to form a won ton.

4 Drop the dumplings into a large pan of boiling water and cook for 5 minutes.

5 To serve, assemble 4 or 5 pieces per serving on a small plate and pour over a generous amount of the sauce.

Overleaf *The Great Wall of China still stretches right across the north of the country*

soy chicken wings
si yau gai yik

Everyone loves this dish. It is simple to prepare but highly aromatic and rich in taste. Frozen chicken wings can be used instead of fresh ones.

SERVES 3–4

9 oz/250 g chicken wings, defrosted if frozen

1 cup water

1 tbsp sliced scallion

1-inch/2.5-cm piece of fresh gingerroot,
   cut into 4 slices

2 tbsp light soy sauce

1/2 tsp dark soy sauce

1 star anise

1 tsp sugar

1 Wash and dry the chicken wings. In a small pan, bring the water to a boil, then add the chicken, scallion, and ginger and bring back to a boil.

2 Add the remaining ingredients, then cover and simmer for 30 minutes.

3 Remove the chicken wings from any remaining liquid and serve hot.

whitebait with green chili

laat mei baat faan yu

*The silver fish traditionally used in this Sichuan dish
are in the same family as whitebait.*

SERVES 4

6 oz/175 g whitebait*

for the sauce

1 tbsp vegetable or peanut oil

1 large fresh green chili

2 drops of sesame oil

1 tbsp light soy sauce

pinch of salt

pinch of sugar

1 garlic clove, finely chopped

1 In a large pan of boiling water, cook the fish for
30 seconds–2 minutes, or until the flesh is turning
soft but not breaking up. Drain, then set aside and cool.

2 To prepare the sauce, first heat the oil in a small
pan and when smoking, cook the chili until the skin
blisters. Remove the skin and finely chop the chili.
When cool, mix with all the other ingredients.

3 To serve, pour the sauce over the fish and serve
immediately.

*cook's tip
The fish have a tendency to stick together and break
easily once cooked, so treat with care.

tea-scented eggs
cha yip daan

This dish is a common street food in China. Vendors often keep the eggs in hot water for a long time, turning the yolk rather gray. This version beautifully marbles the egg white but keeps the yolk yellow.

SERVES 6
6 eggs*
generous 2 cups water
2 tbsp black tea leaves

1 Bring a pan of water to a boil and cook the eggs for 10 minutes. Remove the eggs from the pan and lightly crack the shells with the back of a spoon.

2 Bring the water back to a boil and simmer the tea leaves for 5 minutes. Turn off the heat. Place the eggs in the tea and let stand until the tea has cooled.

3 Serve the eggs whole for breakfast or as part of a meal, shelled or, more traditionally, unshelled.

cook's tip
Substitute 12 quail's eggs for a party version.

pickled baby cucumbers
leung bun siu wong gwa

The Chinese cucumbers used for this dish are thin and short, about 7 inches/18 cm long, and are available in Oriental stores. You could also use small Middle-Eastern cucumbers.

SERVES 4

1 tbsp vegetable or peanut oil, for frying

14 oz/400 g baby cucumbers

generous 2 cups white rice vinegar

1 tbsp salt

3 tbsp sugar

3 red Thai chilies, seeded and finely chopped

1 In a wok or deep pan, heat the oil and cook the cucumbers for 3–5 minutes, or until they are bright green. Drain and set aside. When cool, score the skin many times on all sides. Place in a large dish.

2 Combine the vinegar, salt, sugar, and chili and pour over the cucumbers, immersing them in the liquid. Leave for 24 hours*. Serve cold in chunks.

cook's tip
This dish will keep for up to 1 month in the refrigerator.

marinated soybeans
leung bun wong dau

These beans, here cooked and served with their slightly fibrous shells intact, are popped out of their skins to eat. The pungent pickling sauce is made from the lees of Chinese yellow wine. If you can't find any, use Shaoxing rice wine.

SERVES 10–12

8 oz/225 g fresh soybeans, washed and stems
   trimmed with scissors

1¹/₄ cups Shanghai Superior Pickle Sauce

generous ³/₄ cups cold water

3–4 tbsp sugar

1 Bring a pan of salted water to a boil and cook the beans, covered, for about 15 minutes, or until they begin to soften but not open up. Drain and cool.

2 Place the beans in a large bowl and pour over the rest of the ingredients, immersing the beans. Let stand for 24 hours in a cool place*. Serve cold.

*cook's tip
This dish will keep for up to 1 week in the refrigerator.

beancurd and bean sprout soup 61
nga choi dau fu tong

A subtle, nutritious, family-style soup.

SERVES 4–6

10 oz/280 g spareribs, cut into small pieces

5 cups water

2 tomatoes, seeded and coarsely chopped

3 thin slices fresh gingerroot

scant 1 cup bean sprouts

2 tsp salt

7 oz/200 g soft beancurd, cut into 1-inch/2.5-cm cubes

1 Bring a pan of water to a boil and blanch the spareribs for about 30 seconds. Skim the water, then remove the ribs and set aside.

2 Bring the measured water to a boil and add the spareribs, tomato, and ginger. After 10 minutes, remove the tomato skins from the water. Add the bean sprouts and salt and cover and simmer for 1 hour. Add the beancurd cubes and simmer for an additional 2 minutes, then serve.

congee with fish fillet
yu pin juk

This is a typical Chinese breakfast dish, usually made in massive quantities and sold in little cafés. It can be made using inferior broken rice and can also be served as a light meal later in the day.

SERVES 6–8

generous 1 cup short-grain rice

scant 3¼ quarts

7 oz/200 g firm white fish fillet, flaked

2 tsp salt

½ tsp white pepper

6 oz/175 g lettuce, finely shredded

2 tbsp finely shredded scallion

2 tbsp finely shredded fresh gingerroot

3 tbsp light soy sauce, to serve

1 Wash the rice and place in a large pan with the water. Cover, and cook for about 2 hours, stirring regularly.

2 Add the fish fillet with the salt and pepper. Stir well, then return to a boil and cook for a couple more minutes.

3 To serve, divide the lettuce, scallion, and ginger between large individual bowls. Pour the congee on top. Finally, sprinkle with 1–2 teaspoons of good-quality soy sauce.

Hong Kong is no less dynamic by night than it is by day

hot-and-sour soup
syun laat tong

Despite its name, this is neither particularly hot nor particularly sour. Nonetheless, it is a really delicious and typical Chinese soup, a version of which is served in almost all Chinese restaurants.

SERVES 4–5

3 dried Chinese mushrooms, soaked in
   warm water for 20 minutes

4 oz/115 g pork loin

1/2 cup fresh or canned bamboo shoots,
   rinsed (if using fresh shoots, boil in water
   first for 30 minutes)

8 oz/225 g firm beancurd

3 3/4 cups chicken stock

1 tbsp Shaoxing rice wine

1 tbsp light soy sauce

1 1/2 tbsp white rice vinegar

1 tsp white pepper*

1 tsp salt

1 egg, lightly beaten

1 Squeeze out any excess water from the mushrooms, then finely slice, discarding any tough stems. Finely slice the pork, bamboo shoots, and beancurd, all to a similar size.

2 Bring the stock to a boil. Add the pork and boil over high heat for 2 minutes. Add the mushrooms and bamboo shoots and boil for an additional 2 minutes. Next, add the Shaoxing, light soy sauce, rice vinegar, pepper, and salt. Bring back to a boil and simmer, covered, for 5 minutes. Add the beancurd and boil, uncovered, for 2 minutes.

3 To serve, rapidly stir in the egg until it has formed fine shreds. Serve immediately.

*cook's tip
The heat in this soup comes from the liberal use of white pepper.

crab and corn soup
hai yung suk mai gang

One of the most popular soups in Chinese take-away restaurants, this soup was created far from China!

SERVES 4

4 oz/115 g fresh or frozen crabmeat

2¹/₂ cups water

15 oz/425 g canned cream-style corn, drained

¹/₂ tsp salt

pinch of pepper

2 tsp cornstarch, dissolved in
   2 tbsp water (optional)*

1 egg, beaten

1 If using frozen crabmeat, blanch the flesh in boiling water for 30 seconds. Remove with a slotted spoon and set aside.

2 In a large pan, bring the water to a boil with the crab and corn and simmer for 2 minutes. Season with the salt and pepper. Stir in the cornstarch, if using, and continue stirring until the soup has thickened. Rapidly stir in the egg and serve.

*cook's tip
Restaurants tend to add cornstarch to thicken the soup, but the cream-style corn kernels usually provide sufficient thickening.

sichuan pumpkin soup 67
chyun mei naam gwa tong

A hearty, country-style soup from Sichuan and a good illustration of the fact that even in this province, famed for its liberal use of chilies and peppers, some dishes are very mild in flavor.

SERVES 4–6

4 cups chicken stock

1 lb/450 g pumpkin, peeled and cut into small cubes

1 tbsp chopped preserved vegetables

1 tsp white pepper

4 oz/115 g any leafy green Chinese vegetable, shredded

1 tsp salt (optional)

1 Bring the stock to a boil, then stir in the pumpkin and simmer for 4–5 minutes.

2 Add the preserved vegetables with the pepper and stir. Finally add the green vegetable and salt, if using. Simmer for an additional minute and serve.

ground beef and cilantro soup

ngau sung yin sai tong

*The pungent aroma and flavor of cilantro leaves,
a must in so much Chinese cooking, if only
as decoration, dominate this dish.*

SERVES 4–6

6¹/₄ cups chicken stock

2 cups ground beef

3 egg whites, lightly beaten

1 tsp salt

¹/₂ tsp white pepper

1 tbsp finely chopped fresh gingerroot

1 tbsp finely chopped scallion

4–5 tbsp finely chopped cilantro, tough stems discarded

for the marinade

1 tsp salt

1 tsp sugar

1 tsp Shaoxing rice wine

1 tsp light soy sauce

1 Combine all the ingredients for the marinade in a bowl and marinate the beef for 20 minutes.

2 Bring the stock to a boil. Add the beef, stirring to break up any clumps, and simmer for 10 minutes.

3 Slowly add the egg whites, stirring rapidly so that they form into fine shreds. Add the salt and pepper and taste to check the seasoning.

4 To serve, place the ginger, scallion, and cilantro in the base of individual bowls and pour the soup on top.

*The Chinese love of water features is often
incorporated in formal designs*

tomato soup with conpoy
yui chyu faan ke tong

Conpoy (dried scallop) is a relatively expensive food item, and an important component of many festive dishes.

SERVES 4–6

10 oz/280 g pork bones

4 cups water

2 tomatoes, seeded and coarsely chopped

1 large potato, coarsely chopped

1–2 pieces of conpoy (dried scallop), soaked
   in warm water for 20 minutes, then shredded*

1 tsp salt

1 egg, lightly beaten

1 Blanch the pork bones in a large pan of boiling water for about 1 minute. Skim the surface, then remove the bones and set aside.

2 Bring the measured water to a boil, then add the pork bones, tomatoes, potato, and conpoy. Cover and simmer for 1 hour.

3 Add the salt, then rapidly stir in the egg to form tiny shreds and serve.

*cook's tip
Conpoy has a strong flavor and aroma, so use sparingly if you are not familiar with it.

This is a very impressive dish to bring to the table, and its rich aroma fills the kitchen.

whole chicken soup
wun teui ching gai tong

SERVES 6–8

3¹/₂ oz/100 g Yunnan ham or ordinary ham, chopped

2 dried Chinese mushrooms, soaked in
   warm water for 20 minutes

³/₄ cup fresh or canned bamboo shoots,
   rinsed (if using fresh shoots, boil in water
   first for 30 minutes)

1 whole chicken

1 tbsp slivered scallion

8 slices fresh gingerroot

8 oz/225 g lean pork, chopped

2 tsp Shaoxing rice wine

3 quarts water

2 tsp salt

10¹/₂ oz/300 g Chinese cabbage, cut into large chunks

Sesame and Scallion Dipping Sauce (see page 29)

1 Blanch the Yunnan ham in boiling water for
30 seconds. Skim the surface, then remove the ham
and set aside. Squeeze out any excess water from the
mushrooms, then finely slice and discard any tough
stems. Chop the bamboo shoots into small cubes.

2 Stuff the chicken with the scallion and ginger.
Put all the ingredients except the cabbage and
Dippping Sauce in a casserole. Bring to a boil, then
lower the heat and simmer, covered, for 1 hour. Add
the cabbage and simmer for 3 more minutes.

3 Remove the chicken skin before serving, then place
a chunk of chicken meat in individual bowls, adding
pieces of vegetable and the other meats, and pour the
soup on top. Serve with the Dipping Sauce.

won ton soup
wun tun tong

Won tons have wider, looser edges than jiaozi dumplings, are cooked and served in chicken stock, and can be enjoyed as an entrée, a snack, or as a soup course.

SERVES 6–8

for the won tons

6 oz/175 g ground pork, not too lean

8 oz/225 g raw shrimp, peeled, deveined, and chopped

1/2 tsp finely chopped fresh gingerroot

1 tbsp light soy sauce

1 tbsp Shaoxing rice wine

2 tsp finely chopped scallion

pinch of sugar

pinch of white pepper

dash of sesame oil

30 square won ton skins

1 egg white, lightly beaten

for the soup

2 quarts/8 cups chicken stock*

2 tsp salt

1/2 tsp white pepper

2 tbsp finely chopped scallion

1 tbsp chopped cilantro leaves, to serve

1 Mix together the filling ingredients and stir well until the texture is thick and pasty. Set aside for at least 20 minutes.

2 To make the won tons, place a teaspoon of the filling at the center of a skin. Brush the edges with a little egg white. Bring the opposite points toward each other and press the edges together, creating a flower-like shape. Repeat with the remaining skins and filling.

3 To make the soup, bring the stock to a boil and add the salt and pepper. Boil the won tons in the stock for about 5 minutes, or until the skins begin to wrinkle around the filling.

4 To serve, put the scallion in individual bowls, then spoon in the won tons and soup and top with the cilantro.

*cook's tip
Use the best chicken stock you have for this dish, definitely not a stock cube, as the broth needs almost to stand alone as a soup.

FISH & SEAFOOD

Cantonese Steamed Fish (see page 82) is one of China's best and most famous culinary achievements. The simplicity of it is alluring, the final dish relying on a combination of careful cooking (think al dente) and an apparently simple dressing: ginger, scallions, soy sauce, and rice wine.

But the real secret is the freshness of the fish. Almost all fish is purchased still swimming strongly, and good Chinese restaurants always have their own fish tank in the kitchen. "Certainly to have a fresh fish and to cause it to become unfresh is a terrible act," recorded one writer in the Ching dynasty. Steamed fish is always cooked whole and the most delicious part of the fish is deemed to be the soft, sweet flesh of the cheeks, which is usually served by the host to an honored guest. The arrival of a large garoupa, the king of fish for the Cantonese, is usually the highlight of a meal or banquet.

Steaming is perfect for fish since the flesh is quite delicate, but fish can also be flash-fried, perhaps in a touch of batter, gently pan-fried, or braised. Prior to braising, the fish would normally be flash-fried to help it retain its shape.

Seafood such as abalone is fêted not for its crispness or softness but for its chewiness, a concept not all non-Chinese can appreciate. Similarly, sea cucumber (bêche-de-mer) seems to be something of an acquired taste, but is considered a sought-after delicacy, the best coming from Shandong Province. Oysters are more universally liked, but are rarely eaten fresh by the Chinese outside the coastal areas. Dried oysters can be boiled, and the cooking liquid then transformed into the highly flavored oyster sauce so popular in Cantonese cooking.

Right *A peaceful pond at Yu Yuan Gardens, Shanghai*

Shark's fin, now rather controversial in some quarters, is the most prestigious soup ingredient and is a must at Lunar New Year dinners

All kinds of fish and shellfish are salted and dried and need to be reconstituted with water before use. Southern China is most famous for its salted fish, and the aroma in the stores specializing in such products is indeed intense! Salt fish might be flaked into fried rice, while conpoy (dried scallop) is a very important addition to soup.

Shark's fin, now rather controversial in some quarters, is the most prestigious soup ingredient and is a must at Lunar New Year dinners, lavish banquets, and important business occasions. Lobster is well-loved though very expensive, but shrimp, mussels, clams, crabs, and scallops feature heavily. The cooking principle for shellfish is not dissimilar to that for fish: steaming or frying for the minimum amount of time to render the flesh al dente rather than flabby. Flavorings are versatile: for example, scallops can be spiced up or simply stir-fried with vegetables.

In spite of China's long coastline, river fish are more highly prized than those of the sea, and this is also true of so-called seafood, such as shrimp and crabs. The freshwater catch is considered more fine and delicate than saltwater species. The picturesque city of Hangzhou, near Shanghai, is home to the West Lake, which is particularly famous for its fish and shellfish. But landlocked Sichuan Province and the lakes of isolated Yunnan Province, as well as southernmost Guangdong Province, are also great sources of numerous delicacies. Fish is far more commonly eaten in China than meat, and thus represents an important protein source. The most

common varieties are carp and bream, though there are plenty of fish to be seen at the markets that appear to have no obvious Western counterpart and thus no recognizable name.

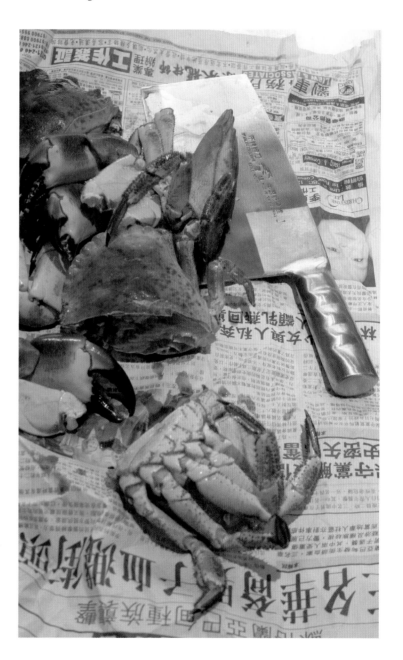

Overleaf The impressive Terracotta Soldiers from the Tomb of Qin Shihuang near Xian

cantonese steamed fish
ching jing yu

The Cantonese are famous for preparing the best steamed fish in the whole of China.

Stalls in the Central Covered Market, Tainan

SERVES 4–6

1 whole sea bass or similar, weighing 1–1 1/2 lb/
   450–675 g, gutted*

1/2 tsp salt

2-inch/5-cm piece of fresh gingerroot, julienned

1 tsp Shaoxing rice wine

1 tbsp slivered scallion

1 tbsp vegetable or peanut oil

1 tbsp light soy sauce

1 To prepare the fish, clean and dry thoroughly. Score the fish on both sides with deep, diagonal cuts. Press the salt into the skin. Set aside for 20 minutes.

2 Place the fish on a plate and top with the ginger, Shaoxing, and half the scallion. Steam in a steamer for 8–10 minutes.

3 Heat the oil in a small pan until smoking and pour over the remaining scallion. Pour this over the fish together with the light soy sauce and serve.

*cook's tip
In China, fish is always served very fresh, complete with tail and head. The fish cheeks are reserved for the most important guest at a meal and are believed to be the sweetest and best part of the fish.

deep-fried river fish with chili bean sauce
dau faan yu

Sichuan Province is criss-crossed by a series of rivers, and river fish are extremely popular. Fish from the sea can be substituted.

1 To prepare the fish, clean and dry thoroughly. Mix together the flour, salt, and water to create a light batter. Coat the fish.

2 Heat enough oil for deep-frying in a wok, deep-fat fryer or large heavy-bottom pan until it reaches 350–375°F/180–190°C, or until a cube of bread browns in 30 seconds. Deep-fry the fish on one side at a time until the skin is crisp and golden brown. Drain, then set aside and keep warm.

3 To make the sauce, first heat all but 1 tablespoon of the oil in a small pan and, when smoking, pour over the dried chili flakes. Set aside.

4 In a preheated wok or deep pan, heat the remaining oil and stir-fry the garlic and ginger until fragrant. Stir in the chili bean sauce, then add the oil-chili flake mixture. Season with the pepper, sugar, and vinegar. Turn off the heat and stir in the scallion. Tip over the fish and serve immediately.

*cook's tip
The best brand of Sichuan broad bean and chili paste is from Bei Yuan (the name is printed on the packet), but other chili bean pastes can be used.

SERVES 4–6

1 whole freshwater fish, such as trout or carp, weighing 14 oz/400 g, gutted

1 heaped tbsp all-purpose flour

pinch of salt

scant 1/2 cup water

vegetable or peanut oil, for deep-frying

for the sauce

scant 1/2 cup vegetable or peanut oil

1 tsp dried chili flakes

1 garlic clove, finely chopped

1 tsp finely chopped fresh gingerroot

1 tbsp chili bean sauce*

1/2 tsp white pepper

2 tsp sugar

1 tbsp white rice vinegar

1 tsp finely chopped scallion

five-willow fish
m lau yu

The name of this fish dish is said to derive from the five vegetables that are shredded, like willow branches, to help create what is basically a sweet-and-sour sauce, though quite subtle in execution.

1 To prepare the fish, clean and dry thoroughly. Score the fish on both sides with deep, diagonal cuts. Press 1/2 teaspoon of the salt into the skin.

2 In a preheated wok or deep pan, heat 4 tablespoons of the oil and cook the fish for about 4 minutes on each side, or until the flesh is soft. Drain, then set aside and keep warm.

3 In a preheated wok or deep pan, heat the remaining oil and stir-fry the ginger, garlic, and scallion* until fragrant. Toss in the vegetables with the remaining salt and stir rapidly for 2–3 minutes. Add the remaining ingredients and mix well for 2–3 minutes. Pour the sauce over the fish and serve immediately.

cook's tip
For a spicy version, add dried red chili, to taste, at the same time as the ginger, garlic, and scallion.

SERVES 4–6

1 whole sea bass or similar, weighing 1–1 1/2 lb/ 450–675 g, gutted

2 tsp salt

6 tbsp vegetable or peanut oil

2 slices fresh gingerroot

2 garlic cloves, finely sliced

2 scallions, coarsely chopped

1 green bell pepper, thinly sliced

1 red bell pepper, thinly sliced

1 carrot, finely sliced

1/2 cup fresh or canned bamboo shoots, rinsed and thinly sliced (if using fresh shoots, boil in water first for 30 minutes)

2 tomatoes, peeled, seeded, and thinly sliced

1 tbsp Shaoxing rice wine

2 tbsp white rice vinegar

1 tbsp light soy sauce

1 tbsp sugar

fried fish with pine nuts

chung ji yu

This recipe is an excellent example of a dish that not only looks very colorful and attractive but also offers a great range of textures.

SERVES 4–6

1/2 tsp salt

1 lb/450 g thick white fish fillets, cut into
   1-inch/2.5-cm cubes

2 dried Chinese mushrooms, soaked in warm water
   for 20 minutes

3 tbsp vegetable or peanut oil

1-inch/2.5-cm piece of fresh gingerroot, finely shredded

1 tbsp chopped scallion

1 red bell pepper, cut into 1-inch/2.5-cm squares

1 green bell pepper, cut into 1-inch/2.5-cm squares

25 g/1 oz fresh or canned bamboo shoots,
   rinsed and cut into small cubes (if using
   fresh shoots, boil in water first for 30 minutes)

2 tsp Shaoxing rice wine

2 tbsp pine nuts, toasted

1 Sprinkle the salt over the fish and set aside for 20 minutes. Squeeze out any excess water from the mushrooms and finely slice, discarding any tough stems.

2 In a preheated wok or deep pan, heat 2 tablespoons of the oil and fry the fish for 3 minutes. Drain and set aside.

3 In a clean, preheated wok or deep pan, heat the remaining oil and toss in the ginger. Stir until fragrant, then add the scallion, peppers, bamboo shoots, mushrooms, and Shaoxing and cook for 1-2 minutes.

4 Finally add the fish and stir to warm through. Sprinkle with the pine nuts and serve.

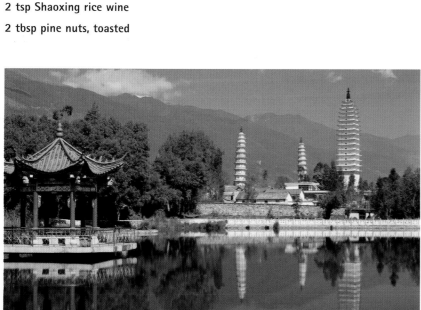

Three pagodas are reflected in the water in a typical Chinese lakeside scene

chilies stuffed with fish paste
yu yuk yeung laat jin

The slight heat of the chilies beautifully complements the aromatic ginger topping.

SERVES 4–6

8 oz/225 g white fish, minced

2 tbsp lightly beaten egg

4–6 mild red and green chilies*

vegetable or peanut oil, for shallow-frying

2 garlic cloves, finely chopped

1/2 tsp fermented black beans, rinsed and lightly mashed

1 tbsp light soy sauce

pinch of sugar

1 tbsp water

for the marinade

1 tsp finely chopped fresh gingerroot

pinch of salt

pinch of white pepper

1/2 tsp vegetable or peanut oil

1 Combine all the ingredients for the marinade in a bowl and marinate the fish for 20 minutes. Add the egg and mix by hand to create a smooth paste.

2 To prepare the chilies, cut in half lengthwise and scoop out the seeds and loose flesh. Cut into bite-size pieces.

3 Spread each piece of chili with about 1/2 teaspoon of the fish paste.

4 In a preheated wok or deep pan, heat plenty of the oil and cook the chili pieces on both sides until beginning to turn golden brown. Drain and set aside.

5 Heat 1 tablespoon of the oil in a wok or deep pan and stir-fry the garlic until aromatic. Stir in the black beans and mix well. Add the light soy sauce and sugar and stir, then add the chili pieces. Add the water, then cover and simmer over a low heat for 5 minutes. Serve immediately.

cook's tip
This dish can also be made with bitter melon (sometimes known as bitter gourd), which should be prepared in the same way as the chilies but blanched before being topped with the fish paste.

steamed sole with black bean sauce
si jap jin taap sa

Even the plainest of fish tastes delicious when steamed with this range of ingredients.

SERVES 3–4

1 sole*, gutted

1/2 tsp salt

2 tsp fermented black beans, rinsed and chopped

2 tsp finely chopped garlic

1 tsp finely shredded fresh gingerroot

1 tbsp shredded scallion

1 tbsp light soy sauce

1 tsp Shaoxing rice wine

1 tsp vegetable or peanut oil

dash of sesame oil

1/2 tsp sugar

pinch of white pepper

1 Place the fish on a plate or create a small dish with foil. Add all the other ingredients on top. Place in a steamer for 10–12 minutes, or until the fish is cooked.

cook's tip
Any white fish is suitable for this dish, and frozen fish can also be used.

A famous Chinese restaurant dish that takes its name from the generous amount of strong alcohol used to "cook" the shrimp.

drunken shrimp
jeui ha

SERVES 4–6

7 oz/200 g raw shrimp, peeled and deveined

1¹/4 cup Shaoxing rice wine

2 tablespoons brandy*

¹/2 tsp salt

1 tbsp finely chopped scallion

1 tsp finely chopped fresh gingerroot

1 Blanch the shrimp in a large pan of boiling water for 30 seconds. Drain and set aside.

2 Combine all the ingredients, then cover and let stand at room temperature for about 1 hour. Strain and serve cold.

*cook's tip
Use a cheap cooking brandy rather than a bottle from the drinks cabinet.

Overleaf The watery landscape of the paddy fields is a familiar view over vast areas of southern China

shrimp fu yung
fu yung ha

An isolated pagoda perched in front of China's Jade Dragon Snow Mountain

Many restaurants now consider this dish too humble to serve, but it makes a great dish for home-cooking.

SERVES 4–6

1 tbsp vegetable or peanut oil

4 oz/115 g raw shrimp, peeled and deveined

4 eggs, lightly beaten

1 tsp salt

pinch of white pepper

2 tbsp finely chopped Chinese chives*

1 In a preheated wok or skillet, heat the oil and stir-fry the shrimp until they begin to turn pink.

2 Season the beaten eggs with the salt and pepper and pour over the shrimp. Stir-fry for 1 minute, then add the chives.

3 Cook for an additional 4 minutes, stirring all the time, until the eggs are cooked through but still soft in texture, and serve immediately.

*cook's tip
Chinese chives are also known as garlic chives and have quite a subtle flavor.

wok-fried jumbo shrimp in spicy sauce

gon jin ha luk

Jumbo shrimp are expensive but highly prized, most often cooked in this kind of manner to impart delicious added flavors while retaining their firm texture.

SERVES 4

3 tbsp vegetable or peanut oil

1 lb/450 g raw jumbo shrimp, deveined but unpeeled

2 tsp finely chopped fresh gingerroot

1 tsp finely chopped garlic

1 tbsp chopped scallion

2 tbsp chili bean sauce*

1 tsp Shaoxing rice wine

1 tsp sugar

1/2 tsp light soy sauce

1–2 tbsp chicken stock

1 In a preheated wok or deep pan, heat the oil, then toss in the shrimp and stir-fry over high heat for about 4 minutes. Arrange the shrimp on the sides of the wok out of the oil, then throw in the ginger and garlic and stir until fragrant. Add the scallion and chili bean sauce. Stir the shrimp into this mixture.

2 Lower the heat slightly and add the Shaoxing, sugar, light soy sauce, and a little chicken stock. Cover and cook for an additional minute. Serve immediately.

cook's tip
Increase the amount of chili bean sauce to create a hotter dish if you prefer.

The many temples, like this one in Shanghai, are places of great solemnity and peace for the Chinese

stir-fried scallops with asparagus
lo seun chaau dai ji

Fresh or frozen scallops are acceptable for this light, refreshing dish. Remove the shells first if you are using fresh scallops.

SERVES 4

8 oz/225 g scallops

2 tsp salt

8 oz/225 g asparagus

3 tbsp vegetable or peanut oil

1/2 cup fresh or canned bamboo shoots,
   rinsed and thinly sliced (if using fresh shoots,
   boil in water first for 30 minutes)

1 small carrot, finely sliced

4 thin slices of fresh gingerroot

pinch of white pepper

2 tbsp Shaoxing rice wine

2 tbsp chicken stock

1 tsp sesame oil

1 Sprinkle the scallops with 1 teaspoon of the salt and let stand for 20 minutes.

2 Trim the asparagus, discarding the tough ends. Cut into 2-inch/5-cm pieces and blanch in a large pan of boiling water for 30 seconds. Drain and set aside.

3 In a preheated wok or deep pan, heat 1 tablespoon of the oil and cook the scallops for 30 seconds. Drain and set aside.

4 In the clean wok or deep pan, heat another tablespoon of the oil and stir-fry the asparagus, bamboo shoots, and carrot for 2 minutes. Season with the remaining salt. Drain and set aside.

5 In the clean wok or deep pan, heat the remaining oil, then add the ginger and stir-fry until fragrant. Return the scallops and vegetables to the wok and sprinkle with the pepper, Shaoxing, and stock. Cover and continue cooking for 2 minutes*, then toss through the sesame oil and serve.

cook's tip
The total cooking time should be no more than 5 minutes.

A man sits behind his boxes of fresh seafood in a Chinese wet market

scallops in black bean sauce
si jap chaau dai ji

Black bean sauce, though strong and aromatic, is a successful match for almost all fish and seafood and is extremely popular in China.

SERVES 4

2 tbsp vegetable or peanut oil

1 tsp finely chopped garlic

1 tsp finely chopped fresh gingerroot

1 tbsp fermented black beans, rinsed and lightly mashed

14 oz/400 g scallops*

1/2 tsp light soy sauce

1 tsp Shaoxing rice wine

1 tsp sugar

3–4 red Thai chilies, finely chopped

1–2 tsp chicken stock

1 tbsp finely chopped scallion

1 In a preheated wok or deep pan, heat the oil. Add the garlic and stir, then add the ginger and stir-fry together for about 1 minute, or until fragrant. Mix in the black beans, then toss in the scallops and stir-fry for 1 minute. Add the light soy sauce, Shaoxing, sugar, and chili.

2 Lower the heat and simmer for 2 minutes, adding the stock if necessary. Finally add the scallion, then stir and serve.

*cook's tip
Fresh scallops, removed from their shells, are always preferable, but frozen scallops work well in this strongly flavored dish.

stir-fried fresh crab with ginger
geung chung chaau hai

Fresh, live seafood, such as the crab used in this recipe, is readily available in many parts of China. Diners enjoy sucking every last little piece of meat from the shell.

SERVES 4

3 tbsp vegetable or peanut oil

2 large fresh crabs*, cleaned, broken into pieces
    and legs cracked with a cleaver

2 oz/55 g fresh gingerroot, julienned

3^1/$_2$ oz/100 g scallions,
    chopped into 2-inch/5-cm lengths

2 tbsp light soy sauce

1 tsp sugar

pinch of white pepper

1 In a preheated wok or deep pan, heat 2 tablespoons of the oil and cook the crab over high heat for 3–4 minutes. Remove and set aside.

2 In the clean wok or deep pan, heat the remaining oil, then toss in the ginger and stir until fragrant. Add the scallion, then stir in the crab pieces. Add the light soy sauce, sugar, and pepper. Cover and simmer for 1 minute and serve immediately.

*cook's tip
This dish can be made only with whole fresh crabs, whether from the sea or freshwater.

clams in black bean sauce
si jap chaau hin 105

The sound of the clam shells hitting the sides of the hot wok make this dish a delight to the ear, as well as to the nose and palate.

SERVES 4

2 lb/900 g small clams

1 tbsp vegetable or peanut oil

1 tsp finely chopped fresh gingerroot

1 tsp finely chopped garlic

1 tbsp fermented black beans, rinsed
   and coarsely chopped

2 tsp Shaoxing rice wine

1 tbsp finely chopped scallion

1 tsp salt (optional)

1 Start by washing the clams thoroughly. Then let the clams soak in clean water until it is time to drain them and toss them in the wok.

2 In a preheated wok or deep pan, heat the oil and stir-fry the ginger and garlic until fragrant. Add the black beans and cook for 1 minute.

3 Over high heat, add the clams and Shaoxing and stir-fry for 2 minutes to mix everything together. Cover and cook for about 3 minutes*. Add the scallion and salt, if necessary, and serve immediately.

*cook's tip
The clams are ready when the shells open. Discard any unopened clams. This dish can also be made with mussels.

A traditional junk plies the waters of Victoria Harbor, Hong Kong

baby squid stuffed with pork and mushrooms
jin yeung cheui tung

Stuffed baby squid are both popular and common in Asia, often sold as a tasty street snack.

SERVES 6–8

14 oz/400 g squid*

4 dried Chinese mushrooms, soaked in warm water
  for 20 minutes

2 cups ground pork

4 water chestnuts, finely chopped

1/2 tsp sesame oil

1 tsp salt

1/2 tsp white pepper

to serve

dark soy sauce

1 red Thai chili, chopped (optional)

1 Clean the squid thoroughly, removing all the tentacles. Squeeze out any excess water from the mushrooms and finely chop, discarding any tough stems.

2 Mix the mushrooms with the pork, water chestnuts, sesame oil, salt, and pepper.

3 Force the stuffing into the squids, pressing firmly but leaving enough room to secure each one with a toothpick.

4 Steam for 15 minutes. Serve with a good soy sauce for dipping, adding the chili to taste.

*cook's tip
Use the smallest squid available, as they are both tender and attractive.

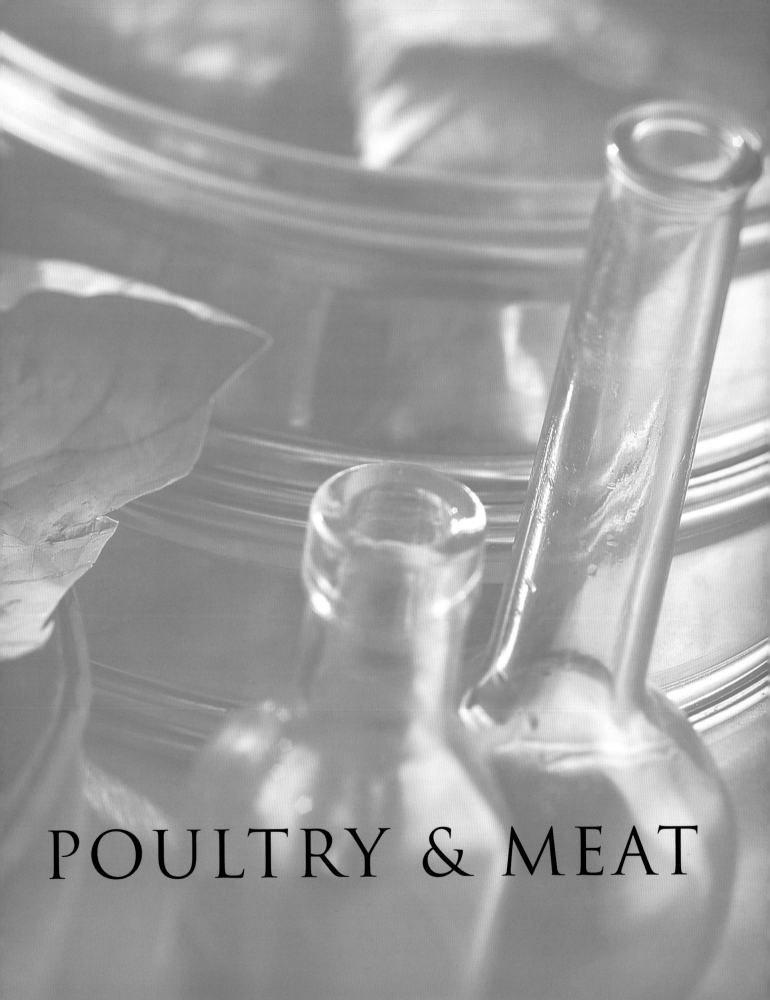

POULTRY & MEAT

Meat for the Chinese is all the better if it is a cut with plenty of fat (pork belly, for example), and comes attached to skin and bone. These three factors are believed to be the foundations for good flavor and, of course, texture. The Chinese are expert at separating the meat from the bone with their teeth, even something as apparently troublesome as a chicken's foot.

The cutting of meat is itself considered an art. There is a proverb that defines the skill of a butcher and surrounds the care he takes of his knife. It is that a good butcher can make a knife last 10 years because he cuts through the bone. A better butcher can make his knife last 20 years because he cuts through the muscle. But the best butcher keeps one knife for his whole lifetime because he cuts between the muscles.

The sharpness of the cleaver and the angle at which the meat is cut make a tremendous difference to the taste and texture of the meat, affecting its propensity to take on the flavor of a marinade or the characteristics of the cooking medium.

Nothing is wasted in the Chinese kitchen, and indeed tongues, ears, feet, and all kinds of offal are highly prized. A pig's trotter would normally be more expensive than a piece of pork loin. Blood is also traditionally incorporated in many dishes. While the practice is less common now, exotic parts of exotic animals can still be sourced in certain markets, particularly in the Cantonese city of Guangzhou in Guangdong Province just north of Hong Kong. Such exotica tend to be more popular with men, as they are believed to have a positive influence on virility.

In China as a whole, pork is the most popular meat, closely followed by chicken. Beef is less common, partly because it is less versatile. In Chinese

Street restaurant in Hsinchu

Right *Fried rice can often be a meal in itself*

Duck is second only to chicken in the Chinese kitchen, and has been almost deified in dishes like Peking Duck

cooking, beef is stir-fried, slow-braised. or ground and added to noodles, with very little in between, in order to prevent it toughening up. Pork and chicken, on the other hand, can be cooked in almost any manner, and pork can even be cooked twice.

In this selection of recipes, chicken runs the gamut from Salt-roasted Chicken (see page 130) to Stir-fried Shredded Chicken with Celery (see page 133) or Chicken with Winter Chestnuts (see page 123).

Duck is second only to chicken in the Chinese kitchen, and has been almost deified in dishes like Peking Duck (see page 165). The white-feathered ducks traditionally used for Peking Duck are partially force-fed, denied too much exercise, and prized for being almost fat-free. Goose, quail, pigeon, and even the tiny seasonal rice-birds, so called because they live in rice paddies in the south of China, are all very popular too. The Cantonese are probably as famous for their roast goose as they are for their steamed fish, restaurants often making their name with this prized dish.

Cattle graze in the grassy northern provinces, where the diet is richer in beef and dairy products. Lamb can also be found, a meat particularly prized by the Muslim communities of Xinjiang. Grilling mutton whole or on kabob sticks are particularly popular cooking methods.

Overleaf *A dramatic hand-painted red poster hung up in Hong Kong*

洽處

上午十一時至
下午四時駕洽
電話六四七八
六三（九龍）

bang bang chicken
pang pang gai

This is a popular dish from northern China, so called because of the traditional tenderizing method whereby the chicken flesh is literally beaten several times! The strong flavor of the sauce is balanced by the freshness of the lettuce.

SERVES 4

12 oz/350 g boneless, skinless chicken meat

few drops of sesame oil

2 tbsp sesame paste

1 tbsp light soy sauce

1 tbsp chicken stock

1/2 tsp salt

pinch of sugar

to serve

8 tbsp shredded lettuce leaves

1 tbsp sesame seeds, roasted

1 Place the chicken in a pan of cold water, then bring to a boil and simmer for 8–10 minutes. Drain and let cool a little, then cut or tear the chicken into bite-size pieces.

2 Mix together the sesame oil, sesame paste, light soy sauce, chicken stock, salt, and sugar and whisk until the sauce is thick and smooth. Toss in the chicken.

3 To serve, put the shredded lettuce on a large plate and spoon the chicken and sauce on top. Sprinkle with the sesame seeds and serve at room temperature.

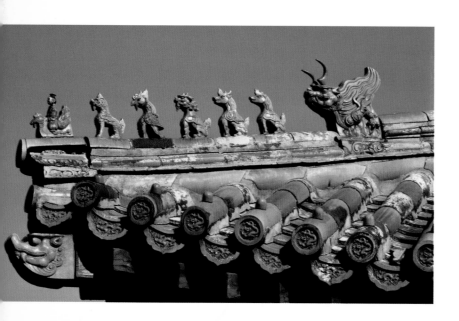

Carved animals ward off evil spirits from a rooftop in China's capital city of Beijing

chicken in guilin chili bean paste
gwai lam laat jeung gai

Guilin is one of the most beautiful tourist attractions in China with its limestone outcrops and scenic river settings. It is not known for its cuisine, but does produce a unique chili bean paste made with yellow beans, a sauce shown off in dishes such as this one.

SERVES 4

1 lb/450 g boneless, skinless chicken meat,
   cut into small chunks

1/2 tsp Sichuan peppers, crushed

1 tbsp light soy sauce

1 tbsp Shaoxing rice wine

1 tsp sugar

vegetable or peanut oil, for deep-frying

2 tbsp Guilin chili bean paste*

2 tbsp finely sliced scallion

chicken stock, if required

1 Marinate the chicken in the peppercorns, light soy sauce, Shaoxing, and sugar. Cover and let stand for at least 30 minutes.

2 Heat enough oil for deep-frying in a wok, deep-fat fryer, or large heavy-bottom pan until it reaches 350–375°F/180–190°C, or until a cube of bread browns in 30 seconds. Deep-fry the chicken pieces for about 3 minutes, or until they are well sealed.

3 In the clean preheated wok or deep pan, heat about 1 teaspoon of the oil and stir-fry the chili bean paste with the scallion until fragrant.

4 Toss the chicken into the wok and stir-fry for about 2 minutes, adding a little hot chicken stock if the pan becomes too dry. Serve immediately.

*cook's tip
Guilin is clearly marked on the label, so this paste is not difficult to find in Asian stores. If you can't find it, you could use another chili sauce instead.

chicken steamed with rice in lotus leaves
ho yip faan

This is a classic Cantonese dish served at a dim sum lunch or breakfast.

SERVES 4–8

4 dried lotus leaves*

generous 2 cups glutinous rice, soaked in cold water
   for at least 2 hours

1³/4 cups cold water

1 tsp salt

1 tsp vegetable or peanut oil

for the filling

3¹/2 oz/100 g raw small shrimp, peeled and deveined

2-inch/5-cm piece of very fresh gingerroot

7 oz/200 g lean chicken meat, cut into
   bite-size strips

2 tsp light soy sauce

2 oz/55 g dried Chinese mushrooms, soaked in
   warm water for at least 20 minutes

1 tbsp vegetable or peanut oil, for frying

7 oz/200 g Cha Siu (see page 148) or pork loin

1 tbsp Shaoxing rice wine

1 tsp dark soy sauce

¹/2 tsp white pepper

1 tsp sugar

1 Soak the lotus leaves in hot water for at least
   1 hour, or until softened. Rinse and dry. Set aside.

2 For the filling, steam the shrimp for 5 minutes.
   Set aside. Grate the ginger on a nutmeg grater,
discarding the fibrous parts on top of the grater and
reserving the liquid that drips through.

3 Marinate the chicken in the light soy sauce and
   ginger juices for at least 20 minutes. Steam for
a few minutes in the marinade. Set aside.

4 Drain the rice and place in a pan with the
   measured water. Bring to a boil, then add the salt
and oil. Cover and cook over the lowest heat for about
15 minutes. Divide into 8 portions and set aside.

5 Squeeze out any excess water from the mushrooms,
   then finely slice and discard any tough stems.
Reserve the soaking water.

6 In a preheated wok or deep pan, heat the oil and
   stir-fry the pork, shrimp, and mushrooms for a
couple of minutes. Stir in the Shaoxing, dark soy sauce,
pepper, and sugar. Add the reserved mushroom soaking
water if the mixture seems dry.

7 Place a portion of rice in the center of each
   lotus leaf and flatten out to form a 4-inch/10-cm
square. Top with the pork mixture and some pieces of
chicken. Top with another portion of rice, then fold
the lotus leaf to form a tight package. Steam for about
15 minutes. Rest for 5 minutes, then serve. This dish
can be eaten straight from the lotus leaf.

cook's tip
While lotus leaves impart flavor as well as aroma,
this dish can be steamed in foil if lotus leaves are
unavailable, or try using a few grape leaves, well rinsed.

san choy bau
saang choi baau

This dish is traditionally made with pigeon, a meat very popular in southern China and Hong Kong, where restaurants often specialize exclusively in pigeon dishes. This is one of the few southern dishes to feature a raw salad vegetable.

MAKES 6

1 tbsp vegetable or peanut oil

3¹/₂ oz/100 g chicken, finely chopped*

1 oz/25 g water chestnuts, finely chopped

1 tsp finely chopped Chinese chives

1 oz/25 g pine nuts, lightly toasted

1 tsp salt

¹/₂ tsp white pepper

6 lettuce leaves, washed

3 tsp plum sauce, to serve

1 In a preheated wok or deep pan, heat the oil and stir-fry the chicken for 1 minute. Add the water chestnuts and chives and cook for 2 minutes. Add the pine nuts and cook for 1 minute. Add the salt and pepper and stir.

2 To serve, place a spoonful in the center of each lettuce leaf, then top with the plum sauce and fold the lettuce leaf to make a small roll.

*cook's tip

You can use ground, rather than chopped, chicken, though the texture is better when the meat is chopped.

chicken with winter chestnuts 123
leut ji man gai

Chicken is one of the most versatile and readily available food items in China and yet retains a festive feel when it is served in a dish such as this.

SERVES 4–6

1 lb/450 g chestnuts*

1 lb 8 oz/675 g chicken meat with skin and bone

1 star anise

1 oz/25 g piece of fresh gingerroot, peeled

2–3 scallions, cut into 2-inch/5-cm lengths

1 cup water

3 tbsp light soy sauce

1 tbsp Shaoxing rice wine

2 tsp dark soy sauce

2 oz/55 g rock sugar

1 Blanch the chestnuts and remove the skins (if they are still in their shells, boil for 30 minutes and remove the shells together with the skins).

2 Cut the chicken into pieces and blanch in a large pan of boiling water for 30 seconds, then drain.

3 Put all the ingredients in a casserole and bring to a boil, then cover and simmer for 45 minutes.

*cook's tip

This dish is only for people who really enjoy chestnuts, as they dominate the flavor and texture.

chicken with cashew nuts

yiu gwo gai ding

This simple but delicious recipe incorporates the main Chinese considerations for a dish: color, flavor, and texture.

1 Marinate the chicken in 2 tablespoons of the light soy sauce, Shaoxing, sugar, and salt for at least 20 minutes.

2 Squeeze any excess water from the mushrooms and finely slice, discarding any tough stems. Reserve the soaking water.

3 In a preheated wok or deep pan, heat 1 tablespoon of the oil. Add the ginger and stir-fry until fragrant. Stir in the chicken and cook for 2 minutes, or until it begins to turn brown. Before the chicken is cooked through, remove and set aside.

4 In the clean wok or deep pan, heat the remaining oil and stir-fry the garlic until fragrant. Add the mushrooms and red bell pepper and stir-fry for 1 minute. Add about 2 tablespoons of the mushroom soaking water and cook for about 2 minutes, or until the water has evaporated. Return the chicken to the wok, then add the remaining light soy sauce and the cashew nuts and stir-fry for 2 minutes, or until the chicken is cooked through.

*cook's tip
The cashew nuts can be roasted in the oven, deep-fried, or toasted in a hot pan.

SERVES 4–6

1 lb/450 g boneless chicken meat, cut into
  bite-size pieces

3 tbsp light soy sauce

1 tsp Shaoxing rice wine

pinch of sugar

1/2 tsp salt

3 dried Chinese mushrooms, soaked in
  warm water for 20 minutes

2 tbsp vegetable or peanut oil

4 slices of fresh gingerroot

1 tsp finely chopped garlic

1 red bell pepper, cut into 1-inch/2.5-cm squares

generous 1/2 cup cashew nuts, roasted*

gong bao chicken
gung bou gai

Also seen on Chinese restaurant menus as Kung Pao Chicken, this is a famous dish from Sichuan, named after a Qing dynasty provincial governor. Because of its Imperial associations, the dish became politically incorrect during the Cultural Revolution, though it is unlikely that anyone takes the same view today.

SERVES 4

2 boneless chicken breasts, with or without skin,
  cut into $^1/_2$-inch/1-cm cubes

1 tbsp vegetable or peanut oil

10 dried red chilies or more, to taste,
  snipped into 2 or 3 pieces

1 tsp Sichuan peppers

3 garlic cloves, finely sliced

1-inch/2.5-cm piece of fresh gingerroot, finely sliced

1 tbsp coarsely chopped scallion, white part only

generous $^1/_2$ cup peanuts, roasted

for the marinade

2 tsp light soy sauce

1 tsp Shaoxing rice wine

$^1/_2$ tsp sugar

for the sauce

1 tsp light soy sauce

1 tsp dark soy sauce

1 tsp black Chinese rice vinegar

a few drops of sesame oil

2 tbsp chicken stock

1 tsp sugar

Part of a highly ornate Chinese temple, surrounded by modern-day tower blocks

1 Combine all the ingredients for the marinade in a bowl and marinate the chicken, covered, for at least 20 minutes. Combine all the ingredients for the sauce and set aside.

2 In a preheated wok or deep pan, heat the oil and stir-fry the chilies and peppers until crisp and fragrant. Toss in the chicken pieces. When they begin to turn white, add the garlic, ginger, and scallion. Stir-fry for about 5 minutes, or until the chicken is cooked.

3 Pour in the sauce, and when everything is well mixed, stir in the peanuts. Serve immediately.

hainan chicken rice

hoi maam gai faan

This dish is originally from semitropical Hainan Island in the south of China, but was introduced by migrants to Singapore, where it is now almost a national dish.

SERVES 4–6

1 chicken, weighing 3 lb 5 oz/1.5 kg

2 oz/55 g fresh young gingerroot, smashed

2 garlic cloves, smashed

1 scallion, tied in a knot

1 tsp salt

2 tbsp vegetable or peanut oil

chili or soy dipping sauce, to serve

for the rice

2 tbsp vegetable or peanut oil

5 garlic cloves, finely chopped

5 shallots, finely chopped

scant 1³/4 cups long-grain rice

3³/4 cups chicken stock

1 tsp salt

1 Wash the chicken and dry thoroughly. Stuff the body cavity with the ginger, garlic, scallion, and salt.

2 In a large pot, bring enough water to a boil to submerge the chicken. Place the chicken in the pan, breast-side down. Bring the water back to a boil, then turn down the heat and simmer, covered, for 30–40 minutes. Turn the chicken over once.

3 Remove the chicken and wash in running cold water for 2 minutes to halt the cooking process. Drain, then rub the oil into the skin. Set aside.

4 To prepare the rice, heat the oil in a preheated wok or deep pan. Stir-fry the garlic and shallots until fragrant. Add the rice and cook for 3 minutes, stirring rapidly. Transfer to a large pan and add the chicken stock and salt. Bring to a boil, then turn down the heat and simmer, covered, for 20 minutes. Turn off the heat and let steam for an additional 5–10 minutes, or until the rice is perfectly cooked.

5 To serve, chop the chicken horizontally through the bone and skin into chunky wedges. Serve with the rice and a chili or soy dipping sauce.

salt-roasted chicken
yip guk gai

This Hakka dish recalls the salt-baked fish of Spain and Portugal, where the salt is the cooking medium rather than a seasoning.

SERVES 6–8

1 chicken, weighing 3 lb 8 oz/1.6 kg

4 lb 8 oz/2 kg coarse salt

for the stuffing

1 scallion, tied in a knot

1-inch/2.5-cm piece of fresh gingerroot, smashed

1 piece of dried tangerine peel

1 Wash the chicken and dry thoroughly. Put the stuffing ingredients into the cavity.

2 In a large casserole, heat the salt, stirring from time to time, for about 5 minutes. When it is hot, make a space at the center for the chicken. Add the chicken and pile the salt on top to bury it. Cover and cook over low heat for 10 minutes.

3 Preheat the oven to 400°F/200°C. Place the casserole in the oven and cook for 45–60 minutes, or until clear juices come out of the chicken into the salt.

4 Remove the chicken from the salt and wash under running hot water. Serve chopped into wedges complete with skin and bone.

stir-fried shredded chicken with celery 133
kan choi chaau gai si

This is Cantonese cooking at its best, where small shreds of chicken cook very quickly in a wok, retaining their juices and texture.

SERVES 4

2 boneless, skinless chicken breasts

1/2 tsp salt

1 tsp light soy sauce

1 tsp dark soy sauce

1 tsp Shaoxing rice wine

1 tsp sugar

3 tbsp vegetable or peanut oil

1 garlic clove, finely sliced

4 thin slices of fresh gingerroot

3 celery stalks, julienned

1 tbsp coarsely chopped scallion,
　cut on the diagonal*

1 Shred the chicken and mix with the salt, soy sauces, Shaoxing, and sugar. Cover and set aside for at least 20 minutes.

2 In a preheated wok or deep pan, heat 2 tablespoons of the oil and stir-fry the chicken until it changes color. Drain and set aside.

3 In the clean wok or deep pan, heat the remaining oil and stir-fry the garlic and ginger until fragrant. Stir in the celery and when it begins to soften, add the scallion and chicken. Cook for 1 minute, and serve.

*cook's tip
Ensure everything is chopped before you begin the cooking process.

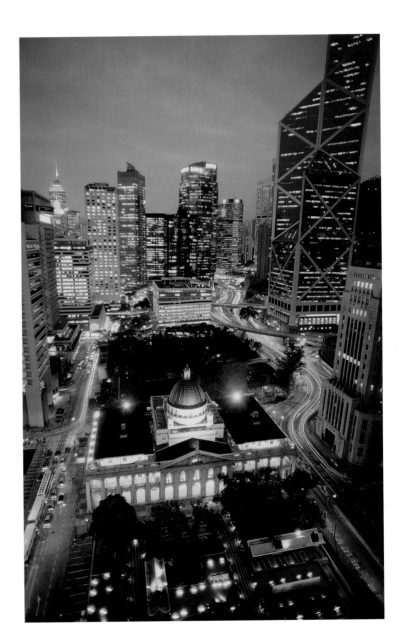

Skyscrapers dwarf government buildings at twilight in Central District, Hong Kong

sweet-and-sour chicken
gu lo gai

SERVES 4–6

1 lb/450 g lean chicken meat, cubed

5 tbsp vegetable or peanut oil

1/2 tsp minced garlic

1/2 tsp finely chopped fresh gingerroot

1 green bell pepper, coarsely chopped

1 onion, coarsely chopped

1 carrot, finely sliced

1 tsp sesame oil

1 tbsp finely chopped scallion

for the marinade

2 tsp light soy sauce

1 tsp Shaoxing rice wine

pinch of white pepper

1/2 tsp salt

dash of sesame oil

for the sauce*

8 tbsp rice vinegar

4 tbsp sugar

2 tsp light soy sauce

6 tbsp tomato ketchup

The Chinese usually associate a sweet-and-sour sauce with fish rather than meat, and would prepare the sauce in a very different way. But this rendering is particularly popular in the West.

1 Place all the marinade ingredients in a bowl and marinate the chicken pieces for at least 20 minutes.

2 To prepare the sauce, heat the vinegar in a pan and add the sugar, light soy sauce, and tomato ketchup. Stir to dissolve the sugar, then set aside.

3 In a preheated wok or deep pan, heat 3 tablespoons of the oil and stir-fry the chicken until it starts to turn golden brown. Remove and set aside.

4 In the clean wok or deep pan, heat the remaining oil and cook the garlic and ginger until fragrant. Add the vegetables and cook for 2 minutes. Add the chicken and cook for 1 minute. Finally add the sauce and sesame oil, then stir in the scallion and serve.

*cook's tip
Vary the amounts of vinegar and tomato ketchup for a stronger or lighter sweet–sour finish.

beef chop suey 137
jaap seui ngau yuk

Chop suey is believed to have been invented in America, possibly when a restaurant ran out of food and had to create a dish using leftovers. Today it has transformed itself into one of the most popular Chinese restaurant dishes.

SERVES 4

1 lb/450 g ribeye or sirloin steak, finely sliced

1 head broccoli, cut into small florets

2 tbsp vegetable or peanut oil

1 onion, finely sliced

2 celery stalks, finely sliced diagonally

2 cups snow peas, sliced in half lengthwise

1/2 cup fresh or canned bamboo shoots, rinsed and julienned (if using fresh shoots, boil in water first for 30 minutes)

8 water chestnuts, finely sliced

4 cups finely sliced mushrooms

1 tbsp oyster sauce

1 tsp salt

for the marinade

1 tbsp Shaoxing rice wine

pinch of white pepper

pinch of salt

1 tbsp light soy sauce

1/2 tsp sesame oil

1 Combine all the marinade ingredients in a bowl and marinate the beef for at least 20 minutes. Blanch the broccoli in a large pan of boiling water for 30 seconds. Drain and set aside.

2 In a preheated wok or deep pan, heat 1 tablespoon of the oil and stir-fry the beef until the color has changed. Remove and set aside.

3 In the clean wok or deep pan, heat the remaining oil and stir-fry the onion for 1 minute. Add the celery and broccoli and cook for 2 minutes. Add the snow peas, bamboo shoots, chestnuts, and mushrooms and cook for 1 minute. Add the beef, then season with the oyster sauce and salt and serve*.

*cook's tip

Most restaurants would use cornstarch to thicken the sauce. This is a fresh-tasting version, and any water from the vegetables is evaporated in the wok.

Skyscrapers tower over the yacht club at Causeway Bay's typhoon shelter in Hong Kong

braised beef with star anise
lou ngau yuk

SERVES 4–6

2 lb 4 oz/1 kg blade or stewing beef*

1 tbsp vegetable or peanut oil

1 garlic clove, finely chopped

1 thin slice of fresh gingerroot, finely chopped

2 star anise

Soy Mustard Dipping Sauce, to serve (see page 29)

for the marinade

2 tbsp light soy sauce

1 tbsp hoisin sauce

3 tbsp Shaoxing rice wine

pinch of salt

pinch of pepper

2 tbsp white rice vinegar

1 tsp sugar

In Chinese cooking, beef is usually either ground or shredded and cooked rapidly, or braised very slowly to prevent the meat toughening up.

1 Combine all the marinade ingredients in a bowl and marinate the beef for at least 2 hours, turning and basting from time to time.

2 Heat the oil in a casserole and stir-fry the garlic, ginger, and star anise until fragrant. Remove the beef from the marinade, reserving the marinade, and over medium heat seal it on both sides.

3 Pour the marinade over the beef. Cover and simmer for about 90 minutes, turning the meat 2 or 3 times and basting from time to time. Insure there is always a little liquid at the bottom of the pan, but not too much, adding hot water if necessary.

4 When cooked, rest the beef for a couple of minutes. Slice thinly and serve hot or cold with the soy mustard dipping sauce.

cook's tip

Meat in a dish such as this would traditionally be pounded and then pricked with a fork to soften the texture and aid marination, but with good-quality meat, this is not necessary.

ma po doufu
ma po dau fu

1 Cut the beancurd into 3/4-inch/2-cm cubes and arrange in a large pan. Pour over enough boiling water to cover and let rest.

2 In a preheated wok or deep pan, heat the oil until almost smoking. Throw in the Sichuan peppers and stir until fragrant. Add the beef and stir-fry until brown and crispy.

3 Lower the heat and add the chili bean sauce and black beans and stir for about 30 seconds, or until the oil is richly red.

4 Pour in the hot chicken stock and gently add the drained beancurd. Season with the sugar, light soy sauce, and salt. Simmer for about 5 minutes.

5 Finally, toss in the scallion. Transfer into 1 large or 4 individual bowls and serve.

This spicy braised beancurd dish is named after the "pockmarked grandmother" who is credited with creating it in the city of Chengdu in Sichuan Province. Legend has it that the meat was added only after one of her customers, a porter, brought a little meat with him and asked her to add it to the pot.

SERVES 4

1 lb/450 g beancurd

2 tbsp vegetable or peanut oil

1 tsp Sichuan peppers

scant 1 cup ground beef

2 tbsp chili bean sauce

1 tsp fermented black beans, rinsed and lightly mashed

1 1/4 cups hot chicken stock

pinch of sugar

1 tsp light soy sauce

pinch of salt

2 tbsp thinly sliced scallion, cut on the diagonal

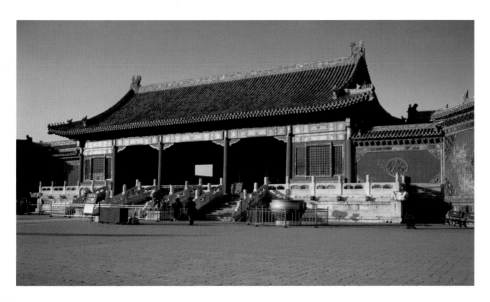

One of the grand entrances through to the Forbidden City in Beijing

Overleaf An urban view of tower blocks and skyscraper offices in Hong Kong

mongolian hot pot
mung gu fo wo

The traditional Mongolian firepot used for this dish is a ring-shaped vessel. It fits over a chimney holding burning charcoal, which heats the water in which the foods are cooked. Hot pots are extremely popular in China, particularly in cold weather. If you don't have a hot pot, you can use a pot set on a hot plate.

SERVES 6

6 dried Chinese mushrooms, soaked in warm water
    for 20 minutes

2^1/$_2$ cups chicken stock

1 lb/450 g lean ribeye or sirloin steak, very finely sliced

1 lb/450 g lean chicken, very finely sliced

8 oz/225 g shrimp, peeled and deveined

1 cup fresh or canned bamboo shoots,
    rinsed and julienned (if using fresh shoots,
    boil in water first for 30 minutes)

1 cup snow peas, trimmed

1 lb/450 g Chinese cabbage, chopped

Dipping Sauces (see page 29)

2 tsp salt

8 oz/225 g beanthread noodles

1 Squeeze out any excess water from the mushrooms and finely slice, discarding any tough stems. Add to the stock.

2 Arrange the meat, shrimp, and vegetables on a platter. Put the dipping sauces in small individual dishes. Bring the stock to a boil in the hotpot and add the salt. Throw in a few noodles and vegetables.

3 To eat, each diner cooks their own food by holding it in the stock with their chopsticks, then dips it in their choice of sauces. When the last foods have been cooked, the soup is served in individual bowls*.

*cook's tip
The fun of this dish is that everyone cooks their own food around the central pot, and the water transforms itself into a delicious soup that can be eaten last.

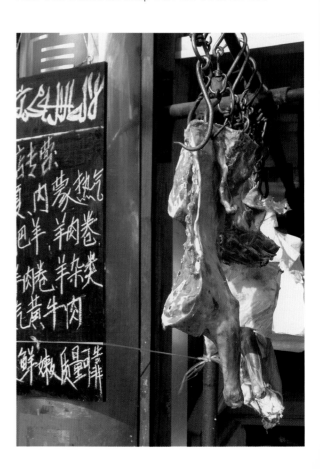

Meat is hung on hooks to be sold in all of China's fresh food markets

stir-fried beef with broccoli and ginger 147
laan fa chaau ngau yuk

This is now a classic combination of flavors and textures and, of course, color.

SERVES 4-6

12 oz/350 g tenderloin steak, cut into thin strips

6 oz/175 g broccoli florets

2 tbsp vegetable or peanut oil

1 garlic clove, finely chopped

1 tsp finely chopped fresh gingerroot

1 small onion, finely sliced

1 tsp salt

1 tsp light soy sauce

for the marinade

1 tbsp light soy sauce

1 tsp sesame oil

1 tsp Shaoxing rice wine

1 tsp sugar

pinch of white pepper

1 Combine the marinade ingredients in a bowl, then mix in the beef. Cover and let stand for 1 hour, basting occasionally. Blanch the broccoli in a large pan of boiling water for 30 seconds. Drain and set aside.

2 In a preheated wok or deep pan, heat 1 tablespoon of the oil and stir-fry the garlic, ginger, and onion for 1 minute. Add the broccoli and stir-fry for an additional minute. Remove from the wok and set aside.

3 In the clean preheated wok or deep pan, heat the remaining oil and stir-fry the beef until the color has changed. Return the broccoli mixture to the pan with the salt and light soy sauce and stir until cooked through. Serve immediately.

The teahouse overlooking the ornamental lake in Shanghai's Yu Yuan Gardens

cha siu
mat jap cha siu

Cha siu is the red lengths of roast honeyed pork that hang in the window of every Cantonese restaurant. It is time-consuming to prepare at home, but it is not difficult to make it well. Most Asian stores carry items such as red fermented beancurd and many kinds of bean sauces, as these are staples rather than exotica.

SERVES 4–6

1 lb 8 oz/675 g pork loin

3 tbsp honey, dissolved in 1 tbsp boiling water

for the marinade

1 tbsp yellow bean sauce, lightly crushed

1 tbsp red fermented beancurd

1 tbsp hoisin sauce

1 tbsp oyster sauce

1 tbsp dark soy sauce

1 tbsp sugar

2 tbsp Shaoxing rice wine

1 tsp sesame oil

1 Combine all the marinade ingredients together. Cut the pork loin lengthwise into 2 pieces. Arrange in a single layer in a dish and pour the marinade over the top. Cover and let marinate for at least 2 hours, basting occasionally.

2 Preheat the oven to 425°F/220°C. On a wire cooling rack, lay out the pieces of pork in a single layer, reserving the marinade. Place the rack over a roasting pan of boiling water and bake for about 15 minutes, insuring that there is always a little water in the pan.

3 Reduce the oven temperature to 350°F/180°C. Turn the strips over and baste with the marinade. Cook for an additional 10 minutes.

4 Remove from the oven and preheat the broiler. Brush the pork with the honey and place under the broiler for a few minutes, turning once. Cool and use as required, cut into chunks, thin slices, or tiny cubes*.

*cook's tip
Cha siu is not usually served on its own, but features in many dishes such as fried rice and stuffings.

lion's head casserole
hung siu si ji tau

The name of this Shanghai recipe follows a Chinese tradition of making dishes sound more elaborate than they really are, or giving auspicious meanings to various dishes. This name is also said to derive from the way in which the meatballs surrounded with cabbage resemble the head and mane of a lion.

SERVES 6

2 oz/55 g dried Chinese mushrooms, soaked for
    20 minutes in warm water

2 oz/55 g raw shrimp, peeled and deveined

4 cups ground pork

3 tsp finely chopped scallion

2 tsp finely chopped fresh gingerroot

1 tbsp light soy sauce

1 tsp sugar

1 tbsp Shaoxing rice wine

3 tbsp vegetable or peanut oil

1 lb/450 g Chinese cabbage leaves, each trimmed
    and cut in half widthwise*

1 tsp salt

1 tsp water

1¼ cups hot chicken stock

1 Squeeze any excess water from the mushrooms and finely chop, discarding any tough stems. Steam the shrimp for 5 minutes.

2 Combine the pork with the scallion, ginger, mushrooms, light soy sauce, sugar, and Shaoxing. Shape into 6 balls with the shrimp at the center of each one.

3 In a preheated wok or deep pan, heat the oil and stir-fry the cabbage with the salt and water for a couple of minutes. Add the stock and meatballs, then bring to a boil and simmer, covered, for 30 minutes over low heat. Serve immediately.

*cook's tip
The cabbage traditionally used for this dish is Tientsin cabbage.

spareribs in a sweet-and-sour sauce
tong chou paai gwat

The genuine sweet-and-sour sauce, on which this version is based, is associated with fish. Here the "new classic" sweet-and-sour sauce, incorporating tomato ketchup and tinned pineapple cubes, is matched with pork.

SERVES 4

1 lb/450 g spareribs, cut into bite-size pieces
   (you or your butcher can cut ribs into pieces
   with a cleaver)
vegetable or peanut oil, for deep-frying

for the marinade

2 tsp light soy sauce

1/2 tsp salt

pinch of white pepper

for the sauce

3 tbsp white rice vinegar

2 tbsp sugar

1 tbsp light soy sauce

1 tbsp tomato ketchup

1 1/2 tbsp vegetable or peanut oil

1 green bell pepper, coarsely chopped

1 small onion, coarsely chopped

1 small carrot, finely sliced

1/2 tsp finely chopped garlic

1/2 tsp finely chopped ginger

3 1/2 oz/100 g pineapple chunks*

1 Combine the marinade ingredients in a bowl with the pork and marinate for at least 20 minutes.

2 Heat enough oil for deep-frying in a wok, deep-fat fryer or large heavy-bottom pan until it reaches 350–375°F/180-190°C, or until a cube of bread browns in 30 seconds. Deep-fry the spareribs for 8 minutes. Drain and set aside.

3 To prepare the sauce, first mix together the vinegar, sugar, light soy sauce, and ketchup. Set aside.

4 In a preheated wok or deep pan, heat 1 tablespoon of the oil and stir-fry the bell pepper, onion, and carrot for 2 minutes. Remove and set aside.

5 In the clean preheated wok or deep pan, heat the remaining oil and stir-fry the garlic and ginger until fragrant. Add the vinegar mixture. Bring back to a boil and add the pineapple chunks. Finally add the spareribs and the bell pepper, onion, and carrot. Stir until warmed through and serve immediately.

*cook's tip
Canned pineapple chunks are the norm, but fresh pineapple is more interesting, if slightly less sweet.

pork ribs braised in soy sauce
hung siu paai gwat

Aromatic and delicious, this dish is a favorite across generations.

SERVES 4

1 lb 5 oz/600 g pork ribs, cut into bite-size pieces

1 tbsp dark soy sauce

1 whole head of garlic

2 tbsp vegetable or peanut oil or shortening

1 cinnamon stick

2 star anise

3 tbsp light soy sauce

2 oz/55 g rock sugar

3/4 cup water

1 Marinate the pork ribs in the dark soy sauce for at least 20 minutes.

2 Break the garlic head into cloves, leaving the individual skins intact.

3 In a preheated wok or deep pan, heat the oil and stir-fry the garlic cloves for 1 minute. Toss in the cinnamon and star anise and stir for an additional minute. Stir in the pork. When the meat is beginning to brown, stir in the light soy sauce, sugar, and water and stir until the sugar is dissolved. Simmer gently, uncovered, for 30 minutes, stirring frequently. Cover and simmer for 60–75 minutes, or until the meat is cooked through and the gravy thick and concentrated*.

*cook's tip
A nice option is to add halved hard-cooked eggs just before the dish has finished cooking.

spicy sichuan pork
wui wo yuk

155

A famous dish from Sichuan Province, this is an excellent way to use leftover plain roasted or boiled pork, recooking it in this medley of flavors.

SERVES 4

10 oz/280 g pork belly, thinly sliced

1 tbsp vegetable or peanut oil

1 tbsp chili bean sauce

1 tbsp fermented black beans, rinsed and lightly mashed

1 green bell pepper, finely sliced

1 red bell pepper, finely sliced*

1 tsp sweet red bean paste (optional)

1 tsp sugar

1 tsp dark soy sauce

pinch of white pepper

1 If cooking the pork especially for this dish, bring a pan of water to a boil and place the pork in the pan, then cover and simmer for about 20 minutes, skimming occasionally. Let the pork cool and rest before slicing thinly.

2 In a preheated wok or deep pan, heat the oil and stir-fry the pork slices until they begin to shrink. Stir in the chili bean sauce, then add the black beans and the red bean paste, if using. Finally, toss in the bell peppers and the remaining ingredients and stir-fry for a couple of minutes.

*cook's tip
Use Chinese leeks instead of bell peppers, if available. Take 2 leeks and finely slice them diagonally.

northern lamb kabobs
bak fong yeung yuk chyun

Northern-style kabobs such as these are traditionally grilled over a charcoal fire and sold by street vendors.

SERVES 3–4

1 onion, finely chopped

10^1/$_2$ oz/300 g lamb or mutton,
   cut into bite-size pieces

1 tsp salt

1 tsp white pepper

1 tsp freshly ground cumin seeds

1 If using bamboo skewers, soak 8 skewers in cold water for 45 minutes to help stop them burning during cooking. Pulverize the onion in a pestle and mortar to release the juices.

2 Mix together the meat and onion, including the onion juices. Cover and marinate for 1–2 hours.

3 Remove as many onion pieces as possible from the meat, then thread the meat onto the skewers and grill or broil for 12 minutes.

4 Just before the meat is cooked, sprinkle with the salt, pepper, and cumin and cook for another 1–2 minutes, or until the meat is slightly crispy on the outside but tender on the inside*.

*cook's tip
Vegetables such as large chunks of onion or red and green bell pepper can be added to the skewers.

xinjiang lamb casserole
san geung yeung naam bou

SERVES 5–6

1–2 tbsp vegetable or peanut oil

14 oz/400 g lamb or mutton, cut into
   bite-size cubes*

1 onion, coarsely chopped

1 green bell pepper, coarsely chopped

1 carrot, coarsely chopped

1 turnip, coarsely chopped

2 tomatoes, coarsely chopped

1-inch/2.5-cm piece of fresh gingerroot, finely sliced

1¹/₄ cups water

1 tsp salt

This famous Xinjiang dish is made in huge quantities and served at festivals. Traditionally, the meat would be cooked in very large pieces and the vegetables added only later. This is a modified version suitable to make for just one family at home!

1 In a preheated wok or deep pan, heat the oil and stir-fry the lamb for 1–2 minutes, or until the meat is sealed on all sides.

2 Transfer the meat to a large casserole and add all the other ingredients. Bring to a boil, then cover and simmer over low heat for 35 minutes.

*cook's tip

Try to cut all the vegetables into pieces about the same size as the meat cubes.

xinjiang rice pot with lamb
san geung yeung yuk faan

SERVES 6–8

2 tbsp vegetable or peanut oil

10 1/2 oz/300 g lamb or mutton,
  cut into bite-size cubes

2 carrots, coarsely chopped

2 onions, coarsely chopped

1 tsp salt

1 tsp ground ginger

1 tsp Sichuan peppers, lightly roasted
  and lightly crushed

generous 2 cups short- or medium-grain rice*

3 3/4 cups water

This wholesome dish from Xinjiang Province is known in Uygur as "poluo rice," which means finger-food. Thus it is eaten with the fingers rather than chopsticks or spoons. This dish is always served at weddings, funerals, and traditional festivals, including the first day of Chinese New Year.

1 In a large casserole, heat the oil and stir-fry the meat for 1–2 minutes, or until the pieces are sealed on all sides. Add the carrot and onion and stir-fry until the vegetables are beginning to soften. Add the salt, ginger, and Sichuan peppers and mix well.

2 Finally, add the rice and water and bring to a boil. Cover the pan and cook over low heat for 30 minutes, or until the rice has absorbed all the water. Serve alone or as part of a meal.

*cook's tip
Use a short- or medium-grain, but not glutinous, rice rather than long-grain rice, to insure that the rice grains stick together a little.

The Singing Sand Dunes of the Gobi Desert

aromatic duck
heung sou ngaap

After chicken, duck is the most popular poultry in China. Because the meat is stronger in taste than chicken, it can be cooked with plenty of warm spices such as cinnamon and cloves for highly aromatic dishes.

SERVES 6–8

1 duck, weighing 4 lb 8 oz/2 kg

1 tsp salt

8 slices of fresh gingerroot

3 scallions

3 cloves

1 stick cinnamon

3 tbsp Shaoxing rice wine

1 tsp sesame seed oil

1 tbsp light soy sauce

2 tsp dark soy sauce

1 oz/25 g rock sugar

1 cup water*

1 Wash and dry the duck, then rub the skin with the salt and set aside for 15 minutes. Rinse well.

2 Stuff the duck with the ginger and scallions, then place it in a casserole and add all the other ingredients. Bring to a boil, then cover and simmer for 1 hour.

3 To serve, cut the duck into chunks and arrange on a plate. Strain the gravy, skimming off any fat, and pour it over the duck pieces.

*cook's tip
Simmer the duck in stock rather than water for an even richer dish.

crispy stuffed duck
baat bou ngaap

This Shanghainese dish is one of many also known as "Eight Treasures," referring to the eight key ingredients in the stuffing.

SERVES 6–8

1 duck, weighing 4 lb 8 oz/2 kg

for the stuffing*

2 oz/55 g laap cheung (Chinese sausage)

2 oz/55 g laap yuk (Chinese bacon)
    or regular smoked bacon

1 oz/25 g dried shrimp, soaked in warm water
    for 20 minutes

2 pieces of conpoy (dried scallop), soaked in warm water
    for 20 minutes

generous 1/2 cup fresh or canned bamboo shoots,
    rinsed (if using fresh shoots, boil in water
    first for 30 minutes)

12 ginkgo nuts, peeled and skinned,
    then boiled for 10 minutes

4 chestnuts, boiled for 10 minutes, then skins removed

2 tsp vegetable or peanut oil

2 oz/55 g lotus seeds, soaked in warm water for 1 hour

2/3 cup glutinous rice, soaked in cold water
    for at least 2 hours, then drained

1/2 tsp salt

1/2 tsp pepper

1/2 tsp sugar

13/4 cups boiling water

1 tbsp light soy sauce

1 To prepare the stuffing, chop the laap cheung and laap yuk into small pieces. Cut the larger shrimp in half and flake the conpoy. Chop the bamboo shoots into small cubes. Halve the ginkgo nuts and finely chop the chestnuts.

2 In a preheated wok or deep pan, heat the oil and stir-fry the lap cheung and lap yuk to release the pork fat, then add the shrimp and conpoy. Next add the bamboo shoots, ginkgo nuts, chestnuts, and lotus seeds. Stir well. Finally add the rice with the salt, pepper, sugar, water, and the light soy sauce. Stir and bring back to a boil, then cover and simmer for 10–15 minutes, or until all the water has been absorbed. Set aside to cool.

3 Preheat the oven to 400°F/200°C. Pack the stuffing into the washed and dried duck and secure the openings with toothpicks or skewers. Roast for 11/2–2 hours, or until the meat is cooked through and the skin is crispy.

*cook's tip
It is worth searching out as many of the correct ingredients for this stuffing as you can, as the result is a very rich and also very unusual blend of flavors and textures.

peking duck
bak ging tin ngaap

SERVES 6–10

1 duck, weighing 4 lb 8 oz/2 kg

3 quarts boiling water

1 tbsp honey

1 tbsp Shaoxing rice wine

1 tsp white rice vinegar

30 Pancakes (see page 30)

1 cucumber, peeled, seeded, and julienned

10 scallions, white part only, shredded

plum or hoisin sauce

The crispy skin is the most highly prized part of the duck. In restaurants, after all the skin has been eaten and the meat has been carved, the carcass is taken back to the kitchen and returns to the table transformed into a soup.

1 To prepare the duck, massage the skin to separate it from the meat*.

2 Pour the boiling water into a large pan, then add the honey, Shaoxing, and vinegar and lower in the duck. Baste for about 1 minute. Remove the duck and hang it to dry for a few hours or overnight.

3 Preheat the oven to 400°F/200°C. Place the duck on a rack above a roasting pan and roast for at least 1 hour, or until the skin is very crispy and the duck cooked through.

4 Bring the duck to the table, together with the cucumber, scallion, and pancakes, and carve off the skin first. On a pancake, arrange a little skin with some cucumber and scallion pieces. Top with a little plum or hoisin sauce, or both. Roll up and eat. Repeat the process with the lean meat.

*cook's tip
To help prepare the skin, insert a bicycle pump in the neck hole and pump until the skin is taut.

This Taoist shrine has a yin and yang symbol at its center, reflecting a belief in the natural course of events

RICE & NOODLES

At banquets, rice is served as the last dish, rather than as an accompaniment to each course. The message is that you fill up on the expensive delicacies such as abalone and shark's fin, and only if you are still hungry, resort to rice. Yet rice also holds an almost mythical status in China, as in other Southeast and East Asian countries.

In reality, in the rice-growing parts of China, rice not only provides a high percentage of daily calories for the bulk of the population, it is the focus of the meal. It serves as a kind of backdrop for a small amount of vegetables or even smaller amount of fish and meat. Sometimes this is necessary, as certain braised dishes can be so rich that they are almost impossible to eat without a lot of rice. But this practice requires that the rice offers taste and aroma, and this, sadly, is less and less often the case. The most popular rice in China is polished long-grain rice, so polished that it loses nutrients contained in the husk, and also flavor. That said, for some, the more neutral the rice backdrop, the better the flavors of the savory dishes come through.

What is frequently referred to as steamed rice is, in fact, boiled rice, and most Chinese kitchens possess a rice cooker dedicated to achieving perfect rice every time. Steaming rice takes far longer than boiling it, though the texture might be a little more fluffy. Steamed rice, in any event, is boiled for a few minutes first. For those who use a pan for boiling rice rather than a cooker, the technique for making Steamed White Rice is explained on page 174.

Egg-fried Rice (see page 175) can almost represent a meal in itself. It is an excellent way to use up yesterday's leftover boiled rice, often combined with other leftovers, although fresh shrimp, chopped

At least as many Chinese who eat rice daily eat noodles, whether these are made from wheat flour, rice flour, or bean flour

Cha Siu (see page 148) and scrambled eggs often appear in the mix, in addition to vegetables or meats.

At least as many Chinese who eat rice daily eat noodles, whether these are made from wheat flour, rice flour, or bean flour. Noodles can be fresh, dried, or semidried. There are a number of key ways to prepare noodles, ranging from soup noodles to fried noodles, braised noodles in a thick gravy, lightly tossed noodles, and cold noodles.

Left People eat on the street on a steep alleyway of teahouses and shops lit by lanterns

Overleaf A woman leads a water buffalo between flooded fields of rice and a field that a boy is using as a swimming hole

Noodles are almost always boiled or soaked in hot water first, then set aside and combined with other ingredients later. Dan Dan Mian (see page 188) from Sichuan Province is one of the most famous noodle dishes in China, while Singapore Noodles (see page 195) is a great example of a dish that left China with Chinese emigrants, underwent some transformations, but still retained its home spirit. Dishes like chop suey or chow mein are usually heavily Westernized versions of Chinese noodles.

The process of preparing noodles can be a great spectacle. Blocks of fresh wheat flour noodle dough are brilliantly separated through swinging the dough by hand into super-long, thin noodles. Chefs also expertly hand cut noodles straight from the block into a pan of boiling water.

steamed white rice
si miu baak faan

The word "steamed" is in fact a misnomer, as the usual method for cooking white rice is to boil it. Different cultures have slightly different techniques, depending on whether the rice grains are to stick together a little, or remain separate. The usual Chinese method is to produce flaky rice.

SERVES 3–4

generous 1 cup rice*

cold water

1 Wash the rice. Place in a pan with the same volume of water plus a little extra (the water should just cover the rice). Bring to a boil, then cover and simmer for about 15 minutes. Turn off the heat and let the rice continue to cook in its own steam for about 5 minutes. At this point, the grains should be cooked through but not sticking together.

***cook's tip*
This recipe is for a standard long-grain rice such as jasmine rice. Allow a little more water and a little more time for basmati.

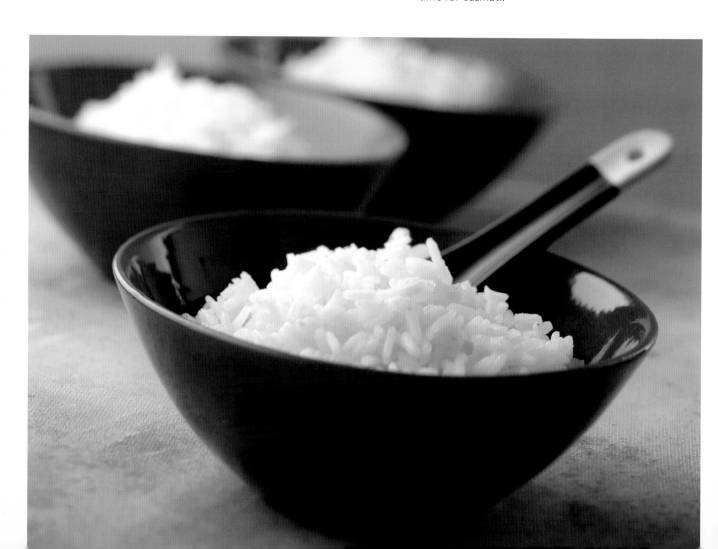

egg-fried rice 175
daan fa chaau faan

The chef who can make the most perfect egg-fried rice is highly esteemed, no matter what else he can cook!

SERVES 4

2 tbsp vegetable or peanut oil

12 oz/350 g cooked rice, chilled*

1 egg, well beaten

1 Heat the oil in a preheated wok or deep pan and stir-fry the rice for 1 minute, breaking it down as much as possible into individual grains.

2 Quickly add the egg, stirring, so as to coat each piece of rice. Stir until the egg is cooked and the rice, as far as possible, is in single grains. Serve the rice immediately.

**cook's tip*
Break up the rice as much as possible after refrigerating it, to make the dish easier to cook.

fried rice with pork and shrimp
yeung jau chaau faan

Fried rice can be so elaborate as to almost constitute a meal in itself, but in China it is often served as the last dish of a meal, just in case diners are still hungry.

SERVES 4

3 tsp vegetable or peanut oil

1 egg, lightly beaten

3 1/2 oz/100 g raw shrimp, peeled, deveined and cut into 2 pieces

3 1/2 oz/100 g Cha Siu, finely chopped (see page 148)

2 tbsp finely chopped scallion

7 oz/200 g cooked rice, chilled

1 tsp salt

1 In a preheated wok or deep pan, heat 1 teaspoon of the oil and pour in the egg. Cook until scrambled. Remove and set aside.

2 Add the remaining oil and stir-fry the shrimp, cha siu, and scallion for about 2 minutes. Add the rice and salt, breaking up the rice into grains, and cook for an additional 2 minutes. Finally, stir in the cooked egg. Serve immediately*.

*cook's tip
There are dozens of variations on the fried rice theme, and almost no rules. Use whatever combination of fresh and leftover food you have.

This is the most basic "fu yung" dish. "Fu yung" indicates that the dish is made with eggs, and here it creates another version of egg-fried rice.

egg fu yung
fu yung daan

SERVES 4–6

2 eggs

1/2 tsp salt

pinch of white pepper

1 tsp melted butter

2 tbsp vegetable or peanut oil

1 tsp finely chopped garlic

1 small onion, finely sliced

1 green bell pepper, finely sliced

1 lb/450 g cooked rice, chilled

1 tbsp light soy sauce

1 tbsp finely chopped scallion

1 cup bean sprouts, trimmed

2 drops of sesame oil

1 Beat the eggs with the salt and pepper. Heat the butter in a pan and pour in the eggs. Cook as an omelet, until set, then remove from the pan and cut into slivers.

2 In a preheated wok or deep pan*, heat the oil and stir-fry the garlic until fragrant. Add the onion and stir-fry for 1 minute, then add the green bell pepper and stir for 1 more minute. Stir in the rice and when the grains are separated, stir in the light soy sauce and cook for 1 minute.

3 Add the scallion and egg strips and stir well, then finally add the bean sprouts and sesame oil. Stir-fry for 1 minute and serve.

*cook's tip
Use a nonstick wok or pan for this dish.

ants climbing a tree
maang ngai seung syu

This simple and hearty family noodle dish is elevated to the poetic with its Chinese name, believed to have been given because the pieces of ground meat, which cling to the noodles, look like an army of ants on the move.

SERVES 4–6

1/2 cup ground beef

1/2 cup ground pork

1 tbsp light soy sauce

pinch of salt

1 tbsp vegetable or peanut oil

1 tbsp chili bean paste

1 tsp dark soy sauce

3/4 cup hot chicken stock

5 oz/140 g beanthread noodles, soaked in
   warm water for 20 minutes* and drained

2 scallions, finely chopped

1 Combine the ground meats with 1 teaspoon of the light soy sauce and the salt.

2 In a preheated wok or deep pan, heat the oil and cook the ground meats until beginning to brown. Add the chili paste and stir rapidly. Stir in the dark soy sauce.

3 Pour in the stock, noodles, and remaining light soy sauce. Cover the wok or pan and simmer for about 8–10 minutes, or until the pan is quite dry. Shake the pan but do not stir. Toss in the scallions and serve.

*cook's tip
The dried opaque noodles used here are made from mung beans, and just need to be soaked or fried to reconstitute them. They break easily, so handle them with care.

Trees flourish in the shadow of the spectacular Yellow Mountain in Anhui

beef chow mein

ngau yuk chaau min

There are many variations on this dish, including different kinds of noodles and different kinds of meat or seafood. Any dish with "mein" in the title features noodles.

SERVES 4

10 oz/280 g tenderloin steak, cut into slivers

8 oz/225 g dried egg noodles

2 tbsp vegetable or peanut oil

1 onion, finely sliced

1 green bell pepper, finely sliced

1 cup bean sprouts, trimmed

1 tsp salt

pinch of sugar

2 tsp Shaoxing rice wine

2 tbsp light soy sauce

1 tbsp dark soy sauce

1 tbsp finely shredded scallion

for the marinade

1 tsp light soy sauce

dash of sesame oil

1/2 tsp Shaoxing rice wine

pinch of white pepper

1 Combine all the marinade ingredients in a bowl and marinate the beef for at least 20 minutes.

2 Cook the noodles according to the directions on the package. When cooked, rinse under cold water and set aside.

3 In a preheated wok or deep pan, heat the oil and stir-fry the beef for about 1 minute, or until the meat has changed color, then add the onion and cook for 1 minute, followed by the bell pepper and bean sprouts. Evaporate off any water from the vegetables. Add the salt, sugar, Shaoxing, and soy sauces. Stir in the noodles and toss for 1 minute. Finally, stir in the scallion and serve.

variation

This dish can also be made with crispy noodles, which are flash-fried after they have been boiled.

chengdu noodles in sesame sauce
sing dou ma laat min

For many Chinese provinces, cold dishes are anathema, but in the extreme Sichuan summers, a dish such as this, strongly flavored but not chili-hot, is believed to be instantly cooling for the body.

SERVES 4–6

14 oz/400 g thin wheat flour noodles

1 cup bean sprouts, trimmed

1 tbsp very finely chopped scallion

for the sauce*

1 tbsp sugar

1 tbsp sesame oil

2 oz/55 g sesame paste

1 tbsp chili oil

2 tsp dark soy sauce

1 tbsp black Chinese vinegar

1 Cook the noodles according to the directions on the package. When cooked, rinse under cold water and set aside. Blanch the bean sprouts in a large pan of boiling water for 30 seconds. Drain and set aside.

2 To prepare the sauce, beat all the ingredients together until the sauce is smooth and thick.

3 To serve, toss the noodles in the sauce, stir in the bean sprouts, and sprinkle with scallion.

*cook's tip
Vary the proportions of the sauce ingredients for an even stronger or spicier flavor.

cross the bridge noodles
go kiu mai sin

From Yunnan Province, this dish was originally made with the area's special "rice thread" noodles, made from rice flour. The dish earned its name thanks to a faithful wife who, while her husband was studying for his exams on a small island, would cross the bridge every day to bring him his favorite noodles in chicken broth. To inspire him, she slowly changed the dish every day, adding more and more ingredients.

SERVES 4

10$\frac{1}{2}$ oz/300 g thin egg or rice noodles

7 oz/200 g choi sum or similar green vegetable

generous 2 quarts chicken stock

$\frac{1}{2}$-inch/1-cm piece of fresh gingerroot, peeled

1–2 tsp salt

1 tsp sugar

1 boneless, skinless chicken breast,
   finely sliced diagonally

7 oz/200 g white fish fillet, finely sliced diagonally

1 tbsp light soy sauce

1 Cook the noodles according to the directions on the package. When cooked, rinse under cold water and set aside. Blanch the choi sum in a large pan of boiling water for 30 seconds. Rinse under cold water and set aside.

2 In a large pan, bring the chicken stock to a boil, then add the ginger, salt, and sugar and skim the surface. Add the chicken and cook for about 4 minutes, then add the fish slices and simmer for an additional 4 minutes, or until the fish and chicken are cooked through. Add the noodles and choi sum with the light soy sauce and bring back to a boil. Test for seasoning. Serve immediately in large individual noodle bowls*.

*cook's tip
A combination of meat and fish or seafood, such as pork and fresh shrimp, can be authentically added.

Overleaf Bicycles are one of the most popular ways of getting around in China

dan dan mian
daam daam min

The name of this dish roughly translates as "pole-carrying noodles," referring to the way street vendors would carry these spicy Sichuan noodles in two pots. It is still possible to come across such vendors, though only outside the larger towns.

SERVES 4

1 tbsp vegetable or peanut oil

1 large dried chili, seeded and snipped into 3 pieces

1/2 tsp Sichuan peppers

scant 1 cup ground beef

2 tsp light soy sauce

10 1/2 oz/300 g fine white noodles

1 tbsp roasted peanuts, chopped

for the sauce

1 tbsp preserved vegetables

1/2 tsp Sichuan peppers, lightly roasted and crushed

1 1/4 cups chicken stock*

1 tsp black Chinese vinegar

1 tsp chili oil

1 tsp dark soy sauce

1 tbsp light soy sauce

1 tbsp sesame paste

few drops of sesame oil

2 scallions, finely chopped

1 Heat the oil in a preheated wok or deep pan and toss in the chili and peppers, then add the meat and stir rapidly. When the meat has changed color, add the light soy sauce and continue to cook until the meat is well browned.

2 Carefully mix the sauce ingredients together and pour into 4 noodle bowls.

3 Cook the noodles according to the directions on the package. When cooked, drain and divide among the bowls.

4 Top with the meat mixture, then sprinkle with the roasted peanuts and serve immediately. Mix well before eating.

*cook's tip

This is a quite dry noodle dish. Add more chicken stock if you prefer a greater quantity of sauce.

"Lo mein," as opposed to "chow mein," is a dried egg noodle dish in which the sauce is served on top of a bed of noodles and mixed by the diners themselves. Lo mein is traditionally made with chicken or beef, and served with a soup on the side.

pork lo mein 191
yuk si lou min

SERVES 4–6

6 oz/175 g boneless lean pork, shredded

8 oz/225 g egg noodles

1¹/₂ tbsp vegetable or peanut oil

2 tsp finely chopped garlic

1 tsp finely chopped fresh gingerroot

1 carrot, julienned

4 cups finely sliced mushrooms

1 green bell pepper, thinly sliced

1 tsp salt

¹/₂ cup hot chicken stock

1¹/₃ cups bean sprouts, trimmed

2 tbsp finely chopped scallion

for the marinade

1 tsp light soy sauce

dash of sesame oil

pinch of white pepper

1 Combine all the marinade ingredients in a bowl and marinate the pork for at least 20 minutes.

2 Cook the noodles according to the directions on the package. When cooked, drain and set aside.

3 In a preheated wok or deep pan, heat 1 teaspoon of the oil and stir-fry the pork until the color has changed. Remove and set aside.

4 In the clean wok or pan, heat the remaining oil and stir-fry the garlic and ginger until fragrant. Add the carrot and cook for 1 minute, then add the mushrooms and cook for 1 minute. Toss in the pepper and cook for 1 minute. Add the pork, salt, and stock and heat through. Finally, toss in the noodles, followed by the bean sprouts, and stir well. Sprinkle with the scallion and serve*.

cook's tip
This recipe tosses everything together in the wok to ease serving and reflects normal restaurant practice.

Hong Kong Island and, across the harbor, Kowloon seen from Victoria Peak at night

rice noodles with beef in black bean sauce
si jiu ngau ho

Rice noodles are very soft and absorb flavors beautifully. Here the white of the noodles perfectly contrasts with the vibrant colors of the peppers.

1 Combine all the marinade ingredients in a bowl and marinate the beef for at least 20 minutes.

2 Cook the rice sticks according to the directions on the package. When cooked, drain and set aside.

3 In a preheated wok or deep pan, heat the oil and stir-fry the beef for 1 minute, or until the meat has changed color. Drain the meat and set aside.

4 Pour off any excess oil from the wok and stir-fry the onion and bell peppers for 1 minute. Add the black bean sauce and stir well, then pour in the light soy sauce. Toss the rice sticks in the vegetables and when fully incorporated, add the beef and stir until warmed through. Serve immediately.

*cook's tip
The rice sticks usually available are the Vietnamese *banh*. They are very soft and absorb flavors beautifully.

SERVES 4–6

8 oz/225 g rump steak, finely sliced

8 oz/225 g rice sticks*

2–3 tbsp vegetable or peanut oil

1 small onion, finely sliced

1 green bell pepper, finely sliced

1 red bell pepper, finely sliced

2 tbsp black bean sauce

2–3 tbsp light soy sauce

for the marinade

1 tbsp dark soy sauce

1 tsp Shaoxing rice wine

1/2 tsp sugar

1/2 tsp white pepper

singapore noodles
sing jau chaau mai

This hugely popular noodle dish started off in China, but after arriving in Singapore, it enjoyed the addition of curry spices.

SERVES 4–6

10¹/₂ oz/300 g thin rice vermicelli

3 tbsp vegetable or peanut oil

2 garlic cloves, finely chopped

1 lb 2 oz/500 g small raw shrimp, peeled, deveined and chopped into 2–3 pieces

4 oz/115 g Cha Siu, julienned (see page 148)

1 onion, finely sliced

1 tbsp mild curry powder, such as garam masala

1 green bell pepper, finely sliced

1 tsp sugar

1 tsp salt

1–2 tsp chicken stock

1 tbsp light soy sauce

1¹/₃ cups bean sprouts, trimmed

1 Cook the vermicelli according to the directions on the package. Drain and set aside.

2 In a preheated wok or deep pan, heat 2 tablespoons of the oil. Toss in the garlic and stir-fry until fragrant. Add the shrimp and stir-fry for 1 minute, or until the shrimp are beginning to change color. Add the cha siu and stir-fry for 1 more minute. Remove everything from the wok and set aside.

3 In the clean wok, heat the remaining oil. Add the onion and stir-fry for 1 minute, then stir in the curry powder. Add the bell pepper, sugar, salt, and stock and stir-fry for 2 minutes. Pour in the light soy sauce followed by the vermicelli. Toss well*. Finally, add the bean sprouts and the shrimp–pork mixture. Stir until warmed through, then serve immediately.

cook's tip
To toss the noodles effectively in the minimum time, use 2 wooden spatulas or spoons.

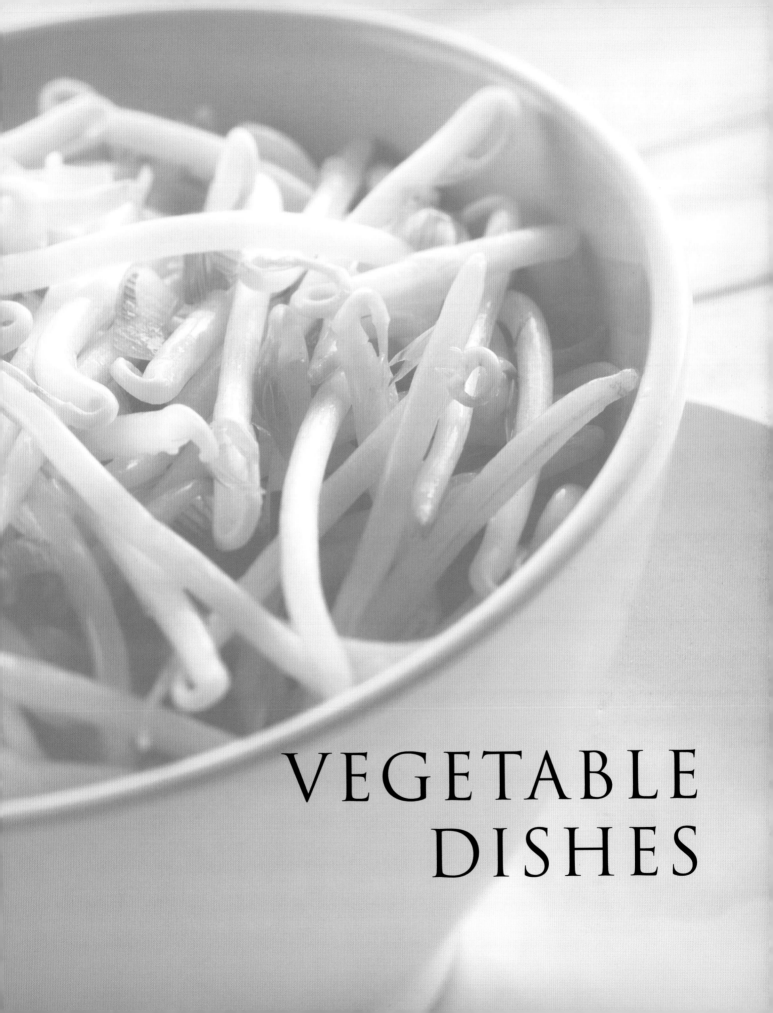

VEGETABLE
DISHES

The Chinese tradition of vegetable or vegetarian cooking developed mostly in the Buddhist monasteries, and is regarded as highly sophisticated. It reaches its heights in Imperial vegetable dishes, while dishes for ordinary people could be resoundingly simple. Dishes are often ascribed fanciful names, along the lines of "Dragon Chasing Phoenix," to belie their humble ingredients.

Beancurd, the dried variety of which is cleverly fashioned into shapes and colors minutely resembling meat, is one of the vegetarian cooking school's most versatile components. Made from yellow soybeans, which are soaked, then crushed and boiled, beancurd is one of the most healthy foods in existence, high in protein, vitamins, and minerals, but free from cholesterol. The traditional Chinese disinterest in dairy products, excluding the Mongolians and Yunnan Muslims, is at least partly to do with the similarly high protein content of beancurd and related products such as soybean milk. The latter is particularly popular for children.

Beancurd was originally a dish for the poor, but is now enjoyed across all social strata, though not everyone enjoys its silky smooth texture. It is believed to have been discovered during the Han dynasty and has a whole folklore surrounding it. An alchemist, determined to create an immortality pill, decided to experiment with the golden soybeans, in the belief that the golden hue might have something to do with longevity. Having soaked and pulped the beans, they simply solidified—into beancurd.

Stir-frying is the favored way to cook vegetables, to the point of al dente. Color is considered very important in vegetable cooking, with red and green bell peppers used to particularly spectacular effect. Green vegetables are always cooked with a little salt

Vegetarianism is followed most often for religious rather than ethical or health reasons, but vegetables are a significant part of every diet

to help them retain their vibrant color. Cutting vegetables into cubes or slivers of a uniform size also contributes to the visual appeal of simple dishes.

Vegetarianism is followed most often for religious rather than ethical or health reasons, but vegetables are a significant part of every diet, whether served alone or in combination with meat, fish, or with the simple addition of chicken stock. Sichuan Fried Eggplant (see page 208) can be cooked with or without the addition of pork meat, and Stuffed Eggplant with Spicy Sauce (see page 211) is, in fact, stuffed with a tiny amount of ground pork. In short, vegetable dishes may include meat, fish, or seafood, while meat, fish, or seafood dishes may include vegetables. The difference is in the proportions.

The vegetable group most likely to be served vegetarian are greens and these are extremely popular—everything from leafy mustard greens or kale to pea shoots, depending on what is in season.

Cabbage is usually stir-fried or braised, but is preserved in the north to provide sustenance during the long, cold winter, eaten in much the same way as *kimchi*. Cabbage is sometimes served cold and raw, though marinated first for a slightly vinegar taste.

Eggs are also very popular, and common, given the large number of poultry reared. Eggs are most usually scrambled and combined with vegetables and beancurd or simply served hard-boiled. Preserved duck eggs are known as one-thousand-year-old eggs, presumably because of the dramatic color transformation that takes place, the yolk turning greenish-black and the white brown-black. These are considered a delicacy and can be eaten alone (excellent with good red wine!) or as part of a dish.

Overleaf *A view across the rooftops of the Forbidden City in Beijing*

braised straw mushrooms
man dung gu

It is worth buying a claypot, a very inexpensive item, as claypot cooking is a great way to treat meat as well as vegetables.

SERVES 4

1 tbsp vegetable or peanut oil

1 tsp finely chopped garlic

6 oz/175 g straw mushrooms, washed but left whole*

2 tsp fermented black beans, rinsed and lightly mashed

1 tsp sugar

1 tbsp light soy sauce

1 tsp dark soy sauce

1 Heat the oil in a small claypot. Cook the garlic until fragrant, then add the mushrooms and stir well to coat in the oil. Add the beans, sugar, and soy sauces, then lower the heat and simmer, covered, for about 10 minutes, or until the mushrooms are soft.

*cook's tip
Unfortunately fresh straw mushrooms are not readily available outside Asia. The canned version is an acceptable substitute. Rinse before use.

A calligrapher paints a message on a scroll in Guangzhou

eggplant with red bell peppers
chou liu ke ji

SERVES 4

3 tbsp vegetable or peanut oil

1 garlic clove, finely chopped

3 eggplants*, halved lengthwise and cut diagonally
   into 1–inch/2.5-cm pieces

1 tsp white rice vinegar

1 red bell pepper, finely sliced

2 tbsp light soy sauce

1 tsp sugar

1 tbsp finely chopped cilantro leaves (optional),
   to garnish

This method of cooking eggplants, incorporating stir-frying and braising, brings a beautiful softness to this dish. It also looks very attractive.

1 In a preheated wok or deep pan, heat the oil. When it begins to smoke, toss in the garlic and stir-fry until fragrant, then add the eggplant. Stir-fry for 30 seconds, then add the vinegar. Turn down the heat and cook, covered, for 5 minutes, stirring from time to time.

2 When the eggplant pieces are soft, add the bell pepper and stir. Add the light soy sauce and sugar and cook, uncovered, for 2 minutes.

3 Turn off the heat and rest for 2 minutes. Transfer to a dish, then garnish with cilantro and serve.

*cook's tip
Use long, thin Asian eggplants, which do not require any salting first.

sichuan fried eggplant
yu heung ke ji

In Chinese, this dish is called "fish fragrant" eggplant. This refers not to fish itself but to the typical blend of ingredients used in Sichuan fish cooking—the garlic, ginger, scallion, and chilies, which is here used to flavor the eggplant.

SERVES 4

vegetable or peanut oil, for frying

4 eggplants, halved lengthwise and cut diagonally into 2-inch/5-cm pieces

1 tbsp chili bean sauce

2 tsp finely chopped fresh gingerroot

2 tsp finely chopped garlic

2–3 tbsp chicken stock

1 tsp sugar

1 tsp light soy sauce

3 scallions, finely chopped

1 In a preheated wok or deep pan, heat the oil and cook the eggplant pieces for 3–4 minutes, or until lightly browned. Drain on paper towels and set aside.

2 In the clean wok or deep pan, heat 2 tablespoons of the oil. Add the chili bean sauce and stir-fry rapidly, then add the ginger and garlic and stir until fragrant. Add the stock, sugar, and light soy sauce. Toss in the fried eggplant pieces and simmer for a couple of minutes. Stir in the scallion and serve.

variation
Ground pork can be incorporated into this dish. Add to the wok before the chili bean sauce and cook until it changes color.

The Great Wall of China is one of the country's most famous tourist attractions

stuffed eggplant with spicy sauce

jin yeung ke ji

The rich batter in which the eggplant is dipped helps prevent the eggplant from absorbing oil during the frying process, leading to a soft and succulent texture.

SERVES 5–6

2 large eggplants, peeled and cut into 1¹/2-inch/ 4-cm wheels

vegetable or peanut oil, for deep-frying

for the batter

²/3 cup besan or gram flour

¹/3 cup all-purpose flour

pinch of salt

1 egg, beaten

1¹/4 cups very cold water

for the sauce

2-inch/5-cm piece of very fresh gingerroot

2 large very juicy garlic cloves

2 tbsp vegetable or peanut oil

3 tbsp chili bean sauce

1 tsp white rice vinegar

2 tsp sugar

²/3 cup chicken stock

for the stuffing

scant 1 cup ground pork

¹/2 tsp very finely chopped scallion

¹/2 tsp very finely chopped fresh gingerroot

dash of Shaoxing rice wine

pinch of white pepper

pinch of salt

1 To prepare the batter, sift together the flours and salt into a large bowl. Stir in the egg, then gradually add the water. Beat for at least 5 minutes, or until the batter is smooth and thick. Rest in the refrigerator.

2 Grate the ginger and garlic for the sauce on a nutmeg grater, discarding the fibrous parts on top of the grater and reserving the liquids that drip through.

3 To prepare the stuffing, mix together all the ingredients and let stand for 20 minutes.

4 Make a small incision—cut less than halfway through—on the side of each eggplant wheel. Stuff about ¹/2 teaspoon of the pork stuffing into the incision, smoothing the surface with a knife to remove any excess.

5 Heat enough oil for deep-frying in a wok, deep-fat fryer or large heavy-bottom pan until it reaches 350–375°F/180–190°C, or until a cube of bread browns in 30 seconds. Dip each eggplant piece into the batter and lower straight into the oil. Cook for about 10 minutes, or until golden brown. Drain and arrange in a bowl or on a serving plate.

6 To prepare the sauce, heat the oil in a preheated wok or deep pan. Add the chili bean sauce and stir for 1 minute, then lower the heat. Stir-fry the ginger and garlic juice for 1 minute, then add the vinegar and sugar and cook for 2 minutes. Finally, add the stock and simmer for 2 minutes. Pour over the eggplant pieces and serve.

spicy green beans
gon bin sei gai dau

This fresh green bean dish from Sichuan Province is one of the region's most famous. It is usually made with a little ground pork, but is at least as delicious when cooked as a vegetable dish.

SERVES 4

generous 1 1/4 cups green beans*, trimmed
　　and cut diagonally into 3–4 pieces

2 tbsp vegetable or peanut oil

4 dried chilies, cut into 2 or 3 pieces

1/2 tsp Sichuan peppers

1 garlic clove, finely sliced

6 thin slices of fresh gingerroot

2 scallions, white part only,
　　cut diagonally into thin pieces

pinch of sea salt

1 Blanch the beans in a large pan of boiling water for 30 seconds. Drain and set aside.

2 In a preheated wok or deep pan, heat 1 tablespoon of the oil. Over low heat, stir-fry the beans for about 5 minutes, or until they are beginning to wrinkle. Remove and set aside.

3 Add the remaining oil and stir-fry the chilies and peppers until they are fragrant. Add the garlic, ginger, and scallion and stir-fry until they begin to soften. Throw in the beans and toss, then add the sea salt and serve immediately.

*cook's tip
The beans can be dry-fried (the most traditional cooking method) or even deep-fried. Boiling or steaming before stir-frying the beans with the other ingredients also works well.

Jade Dragon Snow Mountain, Yunnan Province

stir-fried long beans with red bell pepper
dang lung jiu chaau dau go

Long beans are sold in bunches and differ from green beans in their texture. Though longer and thinner, they retain more crunch even after cooking.

SERVES 4–6
10 oz/280 g long beans*, cut into 2¹/₂-inch/6-cm lengths
1 tbsp vegetable or peanut oil
1 red bell pepper, slivered
pinch of salt
pinch of sugar

1 Blanch the beans in a large pan of boiling water for 30 seconds. Drain and set aside.

2 In a preheated wok or deep pan, heat the oil and stir-fry the beans for 1 minute over high heat. Add the pepper and stir-fry for 1 more minute. Sprinkle the salt and sugar on top and serve.

cook's tip
Long beans are traditionally cooked with egg or black beans or, as in this recipe, a second vegetable that supplies a beautiful color contrast.

stir-fried bean sprouts
ching chaau nga choi

This simple dish is a good accompaniment to rich meat dishes.

SERVES 4

1 tbsp vegetable or peanut oil

generous 1¹/₂ cups bean sprouts*, trimmed

2 tbsp finely chopped scallion

¹/₂ tsp salt

pinch of sugar

1 In a preheated wok or deep pan, heat the oil and stir-fry the bean sprouts with the scallion for about 1 minute. Add the salt and sugar and stir. Remove and serve immediately.

*cook's tip
Stir-fry the bean sprouts over high heat to retain crispness and avoid a watery finish. Serve piping hot.

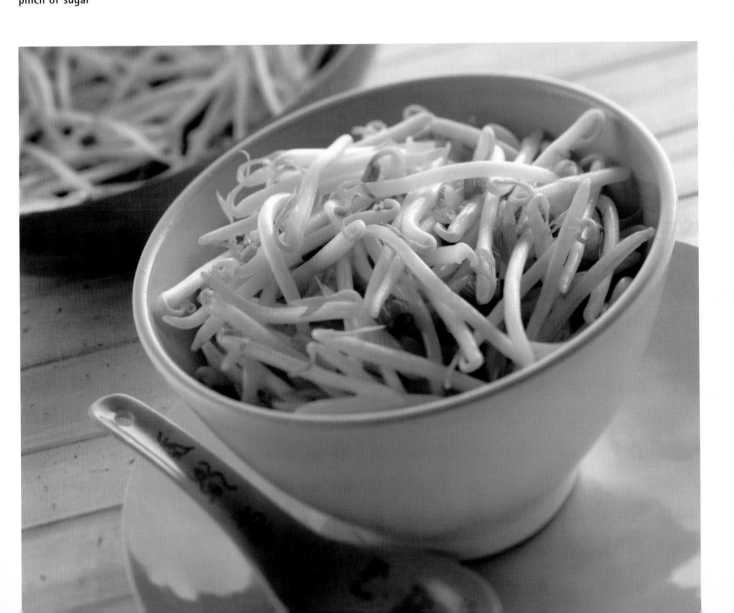

hot-and-sour cabbage
chou liu ye choi

Cabbage, though a relatively recent addition to the Chinese culinary repertoire, works well in stir-fried dishes because this quick cooking method enhances its sweetness while minimizing potentially unpleasant cabbage smells.

SERVES 4

1 lb/450 g firm white cabbage

1 tbsp vegetable or peanut oil

10 Sichuan peppers or more, to taste

3 dried chilies, coarsely chopped

1/2 tsp salt

1 tsp white rice vinegar

dash of sesame oil

pinch of sugar

1 To prepare the cabbage, discard the outer leaves and tough stems. Chop the cabbage into 1¹/4-inch/ 3-cm squares, breaking up the chunks*. Rinse thoroughly in cold water.

2 In a preheated wok or deep pan, heat the oil and cook the peppers until fragrant. Stir in the chilies. Throw in the cabbage, a little at a time, together with the salt, and stir-fry for 2 minutes.

3 Add the vinegar, sesame oil, and sugar and cook for an additional minute, or until the cabbage is tender. Serve immediately.

*cook's tip
Vegetables such as cabbage are not easy to cut into even chunks, but effective stir-frying depends on pieces being as uniform in size as possible.

Overleaf *The dramatic limestone pinnacles of Guilin tower above the Li Jiang River*

stir-fried chinese greens
chaau jaap choi

This is the classic way to cook and serve Chinese green vegetables, served at almost every Cantonese meal.

SERVES 4

1 tbsp vegetable or peanut oil

1 tsp finely chopped garlic

8 oz/225 g leafy Chinese greens, coarsely chopped*

1/2 tsp salt

1 In a preheated wok or deep pan, heat the oil and stir-fry the garlic until fragrant. Over high heat, toss in the Chinese greens and salt and stir-fry for 1 minute maximum. Serve immediately.

*cook's tip

Buy the freshest available of whatever vegetable is in season for the best result.

choi sum in oyster sauce
hou yau choi sam

Oyster sauce is a very popular flavoring and texture in Chinese cooking, particularly in vegetable dishes.

SERVES 4–6

10¹/₂ oz/300 g choi sum*

1 tbsp vegetable or peanut oil

1 tsp finely chopped garlic

1 tbsp oyster sauce

1 Blanch the choi sum in a large pan of boiling water for 30 seconds. Drain and set aside.

2 In a preheated wok or deep pan, heat the oil and stir-fry the garlic until fragrant. Add the choi sum and toss for 1 minute. Stir in the oyster sauce and serve.

*cook's tip
The choi sum can be replaced by other seasonal Chinese greens.

broccoli and snow pea stir-fry
chaau seung cheui

The secret of beautiful Chinese stir-fries is to retain not only the texture but the vivid greens of the vegetables. This is achieved by the addition of a little salt as they cook.

SERVES 4

2 tbsp vegetable or peanut oil

dash of sesame oil

1 garlic clove, finely chopped

8 oz/225 g small broccoli florets

1 cup snow peas, trimmed

8 oz/225 g Chinese cabbage, chopped into 1/2-inch/1-cm slices

5–6 scallions, finely chopped

1/2 tsp salt

2 tbsp light soy sauce

1 tbsp Shaoxing rice wine

1 tsp sesame seeds, lightly toasted

1 In a preheated wok or deep pan, heat the oils, then add the garlic and stir-fry vigorously. Add all the vegetables* and salt and stir-fry over high heat, tossing rapidly, for about 3 minutes.

2 Pour in the light soy sauce and Shaoxing and cook for an additional 2 minutes. Sprinkle with the sesame seeds and serve hot.

*cook's tip
The vegetables shown here are easy to find in markets in the south of China, but almost any vegetables can be incorporated.

bamboo shoots with beancurd
seun jim dau fu

This dish incorporates several of the most typical Chinese ingredients.

SERVES 4–6

3 dried Chinese mushrooms, soaked in warm
   water for 20 minutes

2 oz/55 g baby bok choy

vegetable or peanut oil, for deep-frying

1 lb/450 g firm beancurd, cut into 1-inch/
   2.5-cm squares*

1/2 cup fresh or canned bamboo shoots,
   rinsed and finely sliced (if using fresh shoots,
   boil in water first for 30 minutes)

1 tsp oyster sauce

1 tsp light soy sauce

1 Squeeze out any excess water from the mushrooms
   and finely slice, discarding any tough stems.
Blanch the bok choy in a large pan of boiling water for
30 seconds. Drain and set aside.

2 Heat enough oil for deep-frying in a wok, deep-fat
   fryer or large heavy-bottom pan until it reaches
350–375°F/180–190°C, or until a cube of bread browns
in 30 seconds. Cook the beancurd cubes until golden
brown. Remove, then drain and set aside.

3 In a preheated wok or deep pan, heat 1 tablespoon
   of the oil, then toss in the mushrooms and bok
choy and stir. Add the beancurd and bamboo shoots
with the oyster and soy sauces. Heat through and serve.

*cook's tip
Chill the beancurd first to make it easier to handle.

*A group of men talking outside a building
in the Temple of Heaven complex in Beijing*

scrambled eggs with beancurd
waat daan dau fu

Nutritious and simple, this vegetarian recipe is a typical home-cooked dish.

SERVES 4–6

8 oz/225 g soft beancurd, cut into 1/2-inch/1-cm cubes

4 eggs, beaten

pinch of salt

3 1/2 oz/100 g Chinese chives, finely chopped

1 tbsp Shaoxing rice wine

3 tbsp vegetable or peanut oil

4–5 tbsp vegetable stock*

1 Drop the beancurd into a large pan of boiling water and cook for 2 minutes. Drain and set aside.

2 Combine the eggs with the salt, half the chopped chives, and 1 teaspoon of the Shaoxing.

3 In a preheated wok or large pan, heat 2 tablespoons of the oil and rapidly stir the eggs for 2 minutes, or until they are scrambled. Remove from the heat and set aside.

4 In the clean wok or pan, heat the remaining oil and stir-fry the beancurd cubes for 2 minutes. Add the stock and remaining Shaoxing and simmer for 3 minutes. Add the scrambled eggs and remaining chives and stir. Serve immediately.

*cook's tip
Nonvegetarians might prefer to use chicken stock.

chunky potatoes with cilantro leaves
heung choi tou dau

Potatoes, particularly excellent in Shanxi Province, take a hearty center stage in this simple but delicious modern dish.

SERVES 6–8

4 potatoes, peeled and cut into large chunks

vegetable or peanut oil, for frying

scant 1 cup pork, not too lean,
   finely chopped or ground

1 green bell pepper, finely chopped

1 tbsp finely chopped scallion, white part only

2 tsp salt

1/2 tsp white pepper

pinch of sugar

2–3 tbsp cooking water from the potatoes

2 tbsp chopped cilantro leaves

1 Boil the potatoes in a large pan of boiling water for 15–25 minutes, or until cooked. Drain, reserving some of the water.

2 In a wok or deep pan, heat plenty of the oil and cook the potatoes until golden. Drain and set aside.

3 In the clean preheated wok or pan, heat 1 tablespoon of the oil and stir-fry the pork, bell pepper, and scallion for 1 minute. Season with the salt, pepper, and sugar and stir-fry for 1 more minute.

4 Stir in the potato chunks and add the water. Cook for 2–3 minutes, or until the potatoes are warmed through. Turn off the heat, then stir in the cilantro and serve warm*.

*cook's tip
Serve the potatoes topped with Chinese caviar for an exotic treat.

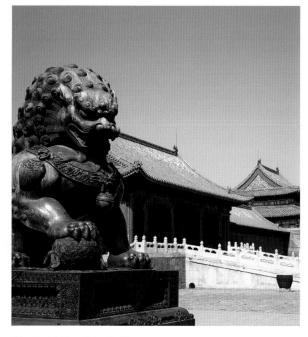

The Forbidden City, Beijing

cabbage and cucumber in a vinegar dressing
bak fong paau choi

There are many chilled northern Chinese dishes. The weather can be so cold that even without refrigeration, food is not spoiled. Serve this dish as part of a cold appetizer selection or as a side dish.

SERVES 4–6

8 oz/225 g Chinese cabbage, very finely shredded*

1 tsp salt

1 cucumber, peeled, seeded, and finely chopped into short thin sticks

1 tsp sesame oil

2 tbsp white rice vinegar

1 tsp sugar

1 Sprinkle the cabbage with the salt and let stand for at least 10 minutes. Drain if necessary. Mix the cabbage with the cucumber pieces.

2 Whisk together the sesame oil, vinegar, and sugar and toss the vegetables in it. Serve immediately.

*cook's tip
The typical cabbage for this dish would be soft-leaved rather than hard.

chinese tomato salad
chung sik faan ke sa leut

Shanxi Province is famous for its tomatoes and vinegar, here combined to create a Western-style salad dish.

SERVES 4–6

2 large tomatoes*

for the dressing

1 tbsp finely chopped scallion

1 tsp finely chopped garlic

1/2 tsp sesame oil

1 tbsp white rice vinegar

1/2 tsp salt

pinch of white pepper

pinch of sugar

1 Mix together all the ingredients for the dressing and set aside.

2 Thinly slice the tomatoes. Arrange on a plate and pour the dressing over the top.

*cook's tip
Use ripe but firm tomatoes and slice very thinly with a very sharp knife.

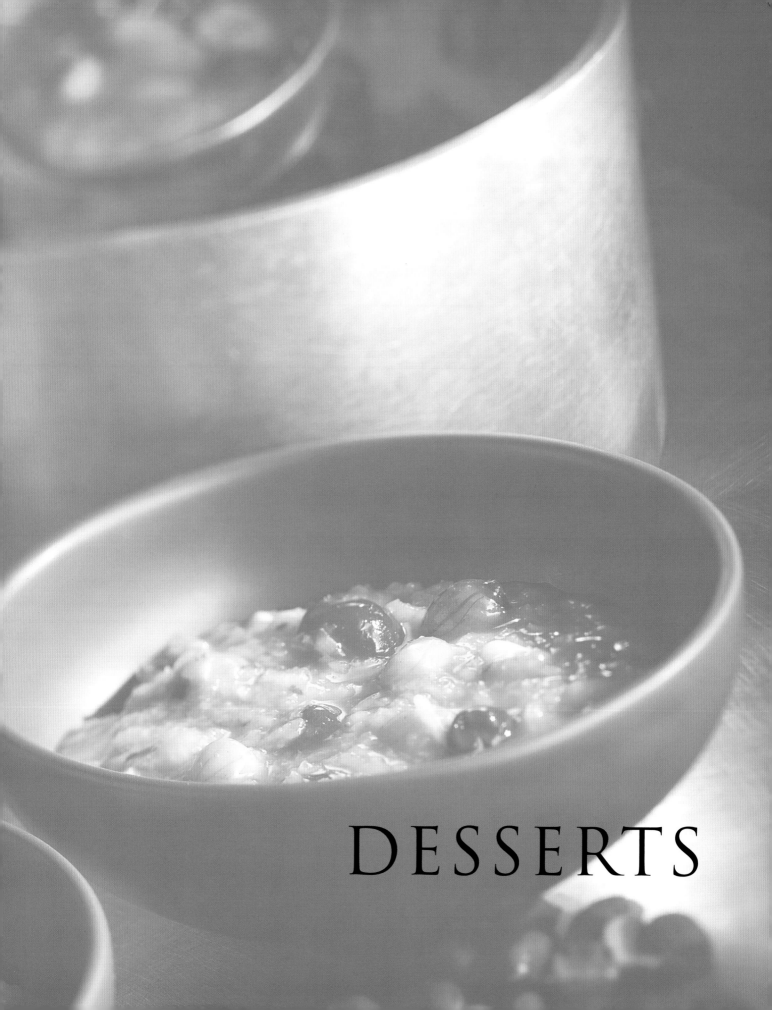

DESSERTS

Dessert after a meal is almost an alien concept in Chinese culinary culture. Its contemporary inclusion after home-cooked meals, or the presence of a dessert selection in Chinese restaurants, represents a Westernization, or at the least an attempt to cater to the demands of Westerners.

This is not to say that the Chinese do not like sweet things. It is just that sweet things are taken separately from a meal or as part of a meal, rather than at the conclusion of it. Dim sum, with its combination of sweet and savory dishes in no particular order, is a good example of this. Dishes are served when they are ready, rather than according to an ordering code. At a Western-style buffet, Chinese guests readily arrange sweet and savory items together on the plate, with no notion of courses.

Sweet items are important at festivals. Perhaps the most famous Chinese cake, the moon cake, is an essential part of the annual midfall festival, where families find a beautiful place from where they can view the full moon. The cake, which is traditionally filled with red bean paste, lotus paste, or sweetened egg yolk, is very sweet and heavy. The cakes are shaped like the moon and stamped with auspicious Chinese characters.

Sweet dishes can also be a result of adding sugar to a savory item: for example, red beans, lotus seeds, and white fungus are all turned into sweet soups when we might normally expect to eat them with salt. Even potato can be turned into a sugary snack.

Other desserts are treated merely as snacks and are available on the streets at almost any time of day. Sweet buns are everywhere and glutinous rice

Right *A man selling snacks to go on the street at one of China's open-air markets*

The most likely dessert is simply fresh fruit, the more seasonal the better, served in chunks without embellishment

flour is used to make delicious little dumplings, which can be steamed in a ginger sauce. Glutinous rice shows up frequently, either steamed into a pudding or cooked in a soup. Dried fruits such as dates, kumquats, and prunes are eaten alone like candies (and may even be salted as well), or incorporated in rice or sweet soup creations.

Certainly baked goods, like fortune cookies, Almond Cookies (see page 252), and all kinds of tarts and pastries, are recent additions to the repertoire, since traditional Chinese kitchens did not have ovens. The use of dairy products can be traced to the Portuguese influence in Macau (and to a lesser extent the British in Hong Kong). In Guangdong Province, sweet, set milk puddings are a favorite and the province's culinary capital of Shunde (where the top Cantonese chefs traditionally hail from) still has little tea shops specializing in these set puddings. Today, French-inspired cakes and gâteaux are favorites for birthdays and other celebrations, although the king of them all is the Portuguese egg tart.

The most likely dessert is simply fresh fruit, the more seasonal the better. Most often it is served in chunks without embellishment, not even sugar, and sometimes a little underripe. Indeed, it would be hard to beat a slice of watermelon or some litchis, still in their hard skins, on a steaming summer's day. And it is worth remembering that fruits such as oranges, persimmons, tangerines, plums, and peaches were all introduced to the West from China.

Overleaf *Fishermen and cormorants ply the waters of the Li Jiang River*

toffee apple slices
bat si ping gwo

This dish can be prepared with bananas and even, as in the north of China, with boiled potatoes.

SERVES 6

4 apples, peeled, cored, and each cut into 8, lengthwise

vegetable or peanut oil, for deep-frying

for the batter

²/3 cup all-purpose flour

1 egg, beaten

¹/2 cup cold water

for the toffee syrup

4 tbsp sesame oil

scant 1¹/4 cups sugar

2 tbsp sesame seeds, toasted

1 To prepare the batter, sift the flour and stir in the egg. Slowly add the water, beating to achieve a smooth and thick batter. Dip each apple slice in the batter.

2 Heat enough oil for deep-frying in a wok, deep-fat fryer or large heavy-bottom pan until it reaches 350–375°F/180–190°C, or until a cube of bread browns in 30 seconds. Deep-fry the apple slices until golden brown. Drain and set aside.

3 To make the toffee syrup, heat the sesame oil in a small, heavy-bottom pan and when beginning to smoke, add the sugar, stirring constantly, until the mixture caramelizes and turns golden*. Remove from the heat, then stir in the sesame seeds and pour into a large flat pan.

4 Over very low heat, place the apple slices in the syrup, turning once. When coated, dip each slice in cold water. Serve immediately.

*cook's tip

Work quickly to insure the syrup does not set and in order to seal the syrup on each apple slice.

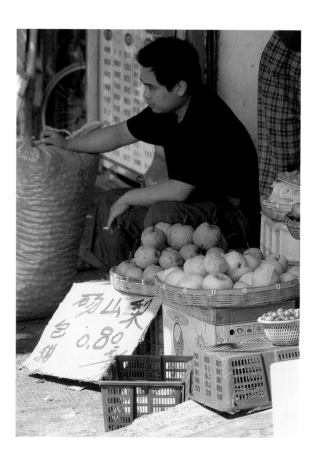

A market fruit-seller waits for customers in front of his small stall

banana fritters
ja heung jiu

SERVES 4–6

vegetable or peanut oil*, for frying

4–5 medium-ripe bananas, halved and cut
into 2³/₄-inch/7-cm long chunks

for the batter

¹/₃ all-purpose flour

pinch of salt

1 egg, beaten

¹/₄ cup milk

2 tablespoons sugar

1 To prepare the batter, sift the flour and salt into
a bowl. Stir in the beaten egg, then gradually add
the milk, beating to create a smooth, thick batter. Stir
in the sugar.

2 Heat some oil in a wok or deep pan. Dip
each banana piece into the batter and cook for
about 3–4 minutes, or until golden brown. Drain and
serve warm.

*cook's tip
Add a little butter to the oil for an even more delicious
result, or even use only butter for frying, taking care
not to burn it.

*Religion is a part of daily Chinese life and shrines
at home and work are filled with burning incense and
food offerings*

mango pudding
mong gwo bou din

Unmistakably Westernized, this dessert from southern China is one of the most accessible Chinese desserts.

SERVES 6

1 oz/25 g sago, soaked in water for at least 20 minutes

1 cup warm water

2 tablespoons sugar

1 large ripe mango, weighing about 10 oz/280 g*

generous 3/4 cup whipping cream

1 tbsp powdered gelatin, dissolved in 1 cup warm water

1 Put the drained sago and warm water in a pan. Bring to a boil and then cook over low heat for 10 minutes, stirring frequently until thick. Stir in the sugar and let cool.

2 Peel the mango and slice off the flesh from the stone. Reduce the mango to a smooth paste in a food processor or blender. Stir in the cream and then the gelatin.

3 Combine all the ingredients. Pour into 6 small bowls and refrigerate until set.

cook's tip
Other soft ripe fruits such as peach can be substituted if mango is not available.

fresh fruit salad with lemon juice
jaap gwo sa leut

SERVES 4–6

2 tbsp sugar

1 lb/450 g mixed melon, cut into balls or cubes*

2 bananas, thinly sliced diagonally

juice of 1 lemon

1 In a large bowl, sprinkle the sugar over the melon pieces. Toss the banana in the lemon juice and add to the melon, then serve immediately.

*cook's tip
Apples, oranges, and grapes, even tropical fruits like mango and litchis, can also be used.

Fresh fruit salad, or a simple platter of fruit wedges, is now the most popular Chinese dessert.

pears in honey syrup
mat jin syut lei

An attractive and delicate dessert of warm fruit in a simple honey syrup.

SERVES 4

4 medium-ripe pears

generous 3/4 cup water

1 tsp sugar

1 tbsp honey

1 Peel each pear, leaving the stem intact. Wrap each in aluminum foil and place in a pan with the stems resting on the side of the pan. Add enough water to cover at least half of the height of the pears. Bring to a boil and simmer for 30 minutes. Remove the pears and carefully remove the aluminum foil, reserving any juices. Set the pears aside to cool.

2 Bring the measured water to a boil. Add any pear juices, the sugar, and honey and boil for 5 minutes. Remove from the heat and let cool a little.

3 To serve, place each pear in a small individual dish*. Pour a little syrup over each and serve just warm.

cook's tip
Serve in small, dark-colored bowls to accentuate the color and shape of the pear.

winter rice pudding with dried fruits
laap baat juk

Folklore says this richly exotic dish, traditionally eaten on the eighth day of the twelfth month of the lunar calendar, was served to condemned prisoners as their last meal before they were executed.

SERVES 6–8

1 tbsp peanuts

1 tbsp pine nuts

1 tbsp lotus seeds

8 oz/225 g mixed dried fruits (raisins, kumquats, prunes, dates, etc.)

generous 2 quarts water

generous 1/2 cup sugar

generous 1 cup glutinous rice, soaked in cold water for at least 2 hours

1 Soak the peanuts, pine nuts, and lotus seeds in a bowl of cold water for at least 1 hour. Soak the dried fruits as necessary. Chop all larger fruits into small pieces.

2 Bring the water to a boil in a pan, then add the sugar and stir until dissolved. Add the drained rice, nuts, and lotus seeds and mixed dried fruits. Bring back to a boil. Cover and simmer over very low heat for 1 hour, stirring frequently*.

*cook's tip

The texture of this dish should be that of a very thick soup. Simply add more water to create a slightly thinner version.

eight-treasures sweet rice cake
baat bou faan

The number eight is considered very lucky in Chinese culture, often thought to represent the eight lotus petals of Buddhism. This attractive dish is traditionally served on festive occasions.

SERVES 6–8

generous 1 cup glutinous rice, soaked in cold
   water for at least 2 hours

1/2 cup sugar

2 tablespoons shortening

2 dried kumquats, finely chopped*

3 prunes, finely chopped

5 dried red dates, soaked for 20 minutes in warm
   water, then finely chopped

1 tsp raisins

12 lotus seeds (if using dried seeds, soak in warm
   water for at least 1 hour)

3 1/2 oz/100 g sweet red bean paste

1 Steam the glutinous rice for about 20 minutes, or until soft. Set aside.

2 When the rice is cool, mix in the sugar and shortening by hand to form a sticky mass.

3 Arrange the dried fruits and seeds in the base of a clear pudding basin. Top with half the rice, then press down tightly and smooth the top.

4 Spread the bean paste on top of the rice, and top with the remaining rice. Press down and smooth the top.

5 Steam for 20 minutes and cool slightly, then turn out onto a plate. Cut into small slices at the table.

*cook's tip
The filling can contain any combination of sweet beans, dates, melon seeds, dried fruits, nuts, etc.

China produces wonderful black and green teas, which are both exported and sold at local markets

almond jelly in ginger sauce 251
geung jap hang yan je lei

The slight bitterness of the ginger sauce works beautifully with the sweet jelly.

SERVES 6–8

for the jelly

3³/4 cups water

¹/8 oz/5 g agar-agar

scant 1¹/4 cups sugar

¹/2 cup evaporated milk

1 tsp almond extract

for the sauce*

3¹/2 oz/100 g piece of fresh gingerroot, coarsely chopped

3³/4 cups water

generous ¹/4 cup brown sugar

1 To prepare the jelly, bring the water to a boil. Add the agar-agar and stir until dissolved. Stir in the sugar.

2 Pour through a strainer into a shallow dish. Pour in the evaporated milk, stirring constantly. When slightly cooled, stir in the almond extract. Refrigerate.

3 To make the ginger sauce, boil the ginger, water, and sugar in a covered pan for at least 1¹/2 hours, or until the sauce is golden in color. Discard the ginger.

4 With a knife, cut thin slices of the jelly and arrange in individual bowls. Pour a little ginger sauce, warm or cold, over the jelly.

*cook's tip
The ginger sauce is also delicious with soft beancurd.

People gather outside the Hall of Prayer for Good Harvests in the Temple of Heaven complex in Beijing

almond cookies
hang yan beng

Almond is very popular as a flavoring in all kinds of Chinese desserts and sweet baked items.

MAKES ABOUT 50 PIECES

4¹/2 cups all-purpose flour

¹/2 tsp baking powder

¹/2 tsp salt

3¹/2 oz/100 g slivered almonds

8 oz/225 g shortening, cut into tiny cubes*

generous 1 cup white sugar

1 egg, lightly beaten

1¹/2 tsp almond extract

50 whole almonds, to decorate (optional)

1 Sift the flour, baking powder, and salt together and set aside.

2 Pulverize the almond slivers in a food processor, then add the flour mixture and pulse until the nuts are well mixed with the flour.

3 Turn the flour and nut mixture into a large bowl, then add the shortening and work into the flour until crumbly. Add the sugar, egg, and almond extract and mix well until the dough is soft and pliable but still firm enough to be handled.

4 Divide the dough into small 1-inch/2.5-cm balls. Place the balls 2 inches/5 cm apart on an ungreased baking sheet and flatten them into circles with the back of a spoon. Press a whole almond into the center of each, if liked.

5 Preheat the oven to 325°F/160°C and bake the cookies for 15–18 minutes, or until just beginning to brown, then remove and turn out onto a cooling rack.

*cook's tip
Butter or margarine can be used instead of the shortening.

Dramatic limestone outcrops and winding rivers are part of the landscape of southern China

Almonds
    Almond Cookies 252
    Almond Jelly in Ginger Sauce 251
Ants Climbing a Tree 178
Apples
    Toffee Apple Slices 240
Aromatic Duck 161
Asparagus
    Stir-fried Scallops with Asparagus 100

Baat Bou Faan 248
Baat Bou Ngaap 162
Baby Squid Stuffed with Pork
    and Mushrooms 106
Bak Fong Paau Choi 230
Bak Fong Yeung Yuk Chyun 156
Bak Ging Tin Ngaap 165
Bamboo Shoots 28
    Bamboo Shoots with Beancurd 225
Banana Fritters 243
Bang Bang Chicken 116
Bat Si Ping Gwo 240
Beancurd 28, 198
    Bamboo Shoots with Beancurd 225
    Beancurd and Bean Sprout Soup 61
    Ma Po Doufu 141
    Scrambled Eggs with Beancurd 226
Bean Sprouts 28
    Beancurd and Bean Sprout Soup 61
    Stir-fried Bean Sprouts 215
Beef 13, 110–13
    Beef Chop Suey 137
    Beef Chow Mein 181
    Braised Beef with Star Anise 138
    Ground Beef and Cilantro Soup 69
    Rice Noodles with Beef in a
        Black Bean Sauce 192
    Stir-fried Beef with Broccoli
        and Ginger 147
Bell Peppers 22, 24, 31, 201
    Eggplant with Red Bell Peppers 207
    Stir-fried Long Beans with
        Red Bell Pepper 214
Black Bean Sauce
    Clams in Black Bean Sauce 105
    Rice Noodles with Beef in a
        Black Bean Sauce 192
    Scallops in Black Bean Sauce 102
    Steamed Sole with Black Bean Sauce 92
Black Beans, Fermented 29
Braised Beef with Star Anise 138

Braised Straw Mushrooms 204
Broccoli
    Broccoli and Snow Pea Stir-fry 222
    Stir-fried Beef with Broccoli
        and Ginger 147

Cabbage 18, 21, 201
    Cabbage and Cucumber in a
        Vinegar Dressing 230
    Hot-and-sour Cabbage 216
Cantonese Steamed Fish 82
Cashew Nuts
    Chicken with Cashew Nuts 125
Celery
    Stir-fried Shredded Chicken
        with Celery 133
Cha Siu 28, 148
Cha Yip Daan 58
Chaau Jaap Choi 220
Chaau Seung Cheui 222
Chengdu Noodles in Sesame Sauce 182
Chestnuts
    Chicken with Winter Chestnuts 123
Cheun Gyun 40
Chicken 17, 18, 22, 110, 113
    Bang Bang Chicken 116
    Chicken with Cashew Nuts 125
    Chicken in Guilin Chili Bean Paste 119
    Chicken Steamed with Rice in
        Lotus Leaves 120
    Chicken with Winter Chestnuts 123
    Gong Bao Chicken 126
    Hainan Chicken Rice 129
    Salt-roasted Chicken 130
    Soy Chicken Wings 56
    Stir-fried Shredded Chicken
        with Celery 133
    Stock 31
    Sweet-and-sour Chicken 134
    Whole Chicken Soup 71
Chili Bean Sauce 28
    Chicken in Guilin Chili Bean Paste 119
    Deep-fried River Fish with
        Chili Bean Sauce 85
Chili Oil 29
Chilies 13, 22, 24
    Chilies Stuffed with Fish Paste 90
    Whitebait with Green Chili 57
Chinese Greens, Stir-fried 220
Chinese Tomato Salad 231
Ching Chaau Nga Choi 215

Ching Jing Yu 82
Choi Sum in Oyster Sauce 221
Choi Yuk Wun Tun 53
Chop Suey, Beef 137
Chopsticks 10, 27, 28
Chou Liu Ke Ji 207
Chou Liu Ye Choi 216
Chow Mein, Beef 181
Chung Ji Yu 89
Chung Sik Faan Ke Sa Leut 231
Chung Sik Yut Naam Cheun Gyun 44
Chung Yau Beng 47
Chunky Potatoes with Cilantro Leaves 229
Chyun Mei Naam Gwa Tong 67
Cilantro 29
    Chunky Potatoes with
        Cilantro Leaves 229
    Ground Beef and Cilantro Soup 69
Clams in Black Bean Sauce 105
Clay Pots 28
Congee with Fish Fillet 62
Conpoy 29, 79
    Tomato Soup with Conpoy 70
Corn
    Crab and Corn Soup 66
Crab 13, 79
    Crab and Corn Soup 66
    Stir-fried Fresh Crab with Ginger 103
Crispy Stuffed Duck 162
Cross the Bridge Noodles 185
Cucumbers 13
    Cabbage and Cucumber in a
        Vinegar Dressing 230
    Pickled Baby Cucumbers 59

Daam Daam Min 188
Daan Fa Chaau Faan 175
Dan Dan Mian 188
Dang Lung Jiu Chaau Dau Go 214
Dau Faan Yu 85
Deep-fried River Fish with
    Chili Bean Sauce 85
Dipping Sauces 29
Drunken Shrimp 93
Duck 21, 24, 113
    Aromatic Duck 161
    Crispy Stuffed Duck 162
    Peking Duck 165
Dumplings in a Cold Spicy Sauce 53

Eggplant 13, 22
    Eggplant with Red Bell Peppers 207
    Sichuan Fried Eggplant 208
    Stuffed Eggplant with Spicy Sauce 211
Eggs 201
    Egg-fried Rice 175
    Egg Fu Yung 177
    One-thousand-year-old 201
    Scrambled Eggs with Beancurd 226
    Tea-scented Eggs 58
Eight-treasures Sweet Rice Cake 248
Equipment 28

Fish 17, 22, 76–9
    Cantonese Steamed Fish 82
    Chilies Stuffed with Fish Paste 90
    Congee with Fish Fillet 62
    Deep-fried River Fish with
      Chili Bean Sauce 85
    Five-willow Fish 86
    Fried Fish with Pine Nuts 89
    Steamed Sole with Black Bean Sauce 92
    Whitebait with Green Chili 57
Five-willow Fish 86
Fresh Fruit Salad with Lemon Juice 245
Fried Fish with Pine Nuts 89
Fried Rice with Pork and Shrimp 176
Fruit 13, 21, 237
    Banana Fritters 243
    Fresh Fruit Salad with Lemon Juice 245
    Mango Pudding 244
    Pears in Honey Syrup 246
    Toffee Apple Slices 240
    Winter Rice Pudding with
      Dried Fruits 247
Fu Yung Daan 177
Fu Yung Ha 96

Gaau Ji 50
Geung Chung Chaau Hai 103
Geung Jap Hang Yan Je Lei 251
Ginger 13, 18, 29
    Almond Jelly in Ginger Sauce 251
    Stir-fried Beef with Broccoli and
      Ginger 147
    Stir-fried Fresh Crab with Ginger 103
Glutinous Rice 30, 234–7
Go Kiu Mai Sin 185
Gon Bin Sei Gai Dau 212
Gon Jin Ha Luk 99
Gong Bao Chicken 126
Green Beans, Spicy 212
Ground Beef and Cilantro Soup 69
Gu Lo Gai 134
Gung Bou Gai 126
Gwai Lam Laat Jeung Gai 119

Ha Do Si 46
Hai Yung Suk Mai Gang 66
Hainan Chicken Rice 129
Hang Yan Beng 252
Heung Choi Tou Dau 229
Heung Chung Bok Beng 49
Heung Sou Ngaap 161
Ho Yip Faan 120
Hoi Maam Gai Faan 129
Hot-and-sour Cabbage 216
Hot-and-sour Soup 65
Hou Yau Choi Sam 221
Hua Jiao 31
Hung Siu Paai Gwat 154
Hung Siu Si Ji Tau 151

Ja Heung Jiu 243
Jaap Gwo Sa Leut 245
Jaap Seui Ngau Yuk 137
Jeui Ha 93
Jiaozi 50
Jiaozi Dipping Sauce 29
Jin Yeung Cheui Tung 106
Jin Yeung Ke Ji 211

Kan Choi Chaau Gai Si 133

Laan Fa Chaau Ngau Yuk 147
Laap Baat Juk 247
Laap Cheung 29
Laap Yuk 29
Laat Mei Baat Faan Yu 57
Lamb 113
    Northern Lamb Kabobs 156
    Xinjiang Lamb Casserole 157
    Xinjiang Rice Pot with Lamb 158
Leung Bun Siu Wong Gwa 59
Leung Bun Wong Dau 60
Leut Ji Man Gai 123
Lion's Head Casserole 151
Lo Seun Chaau Dai Ji 100
Long Beans
    Stir-fried Long Beans with
      Red Bell Pepper 214
Lotus Leaves
    Chicken Steamed with Rice in
      Lotus Leaves 120
Lou Ngau Yuk 138

M Lau Yu 86
Ma Po Dau Fu 141
Ma Po Doufu 141
Maang Ngai Seung Syu 178
Man Dung Gu 204
Mango Pudding 244
Marinated Soybeans 60

Mat Jap Cha Siu 148
Mat Jin Syut Lei 246
Mong Gwo Bou Din 244
Mongolian Hot Pot 144
Mung Go Fo Wo 144
Mushrooms, Dried 29
    Baby Squid Stuffed with Pork
      and Mushrooms 106
Mushrooms, Straw
    Braised Straw Mushrooms 204

Nga Choi Dau Fu Tong 61
Ngau Sung Yin Sai Tong 69
Ngau Yuk Chaau Min 181
Noodles 17, 18, 30, 171
    Ants Climbing a Tree 178
    Beef Chow Mein 181
    Chengdu Noodles in Sesame Sauce 182
    Cross the Bridge Noodles 185
    Dan Dan Mian 188
    Pork Lo Mein 191
    Rice Noodles with Beef in a
      Black Bean Sauce 192
    Singapore Noodles 195
Northern Lamb Kabobs 156

Onion Pancakes 49
Oyster Sauce 30
    Choi Sum in Oyster Sauce 221

Pancakes 30
    Onion Pancakes 49
Pang Pang Gai 116
Pears in Honey Syrup 246
Peking Duck 165
Pepper 30
Pickled Baby Cucumbers 59
Pigeon 113
    San Choy Bau 122
Plum Sauce 30
Pork 22, 25, 110, 113
    Baby Squid Stuffed with
      Pork and Mushrooms 106
    Cha Siu 148
    Fried Rice with Pork and Shrimp 176
    Laap Cheung 29
    Pork Lo Mein 191
    Pork Ribs Braised in Soy Sauce 154
    Soft-wrapped Pork and Shrimp Rolls 44
    Spareribs in a Sweet-and-sour
      Sauce 152
    Spicy Sichuan Pork 155
Potatoes 13, 21, 234
    Chunky Potatoes with
      Cilantro Leaves 229

256

Pumpkin
  Sichuan Pumpkin Soup 67

Restaurants 22–3, 25–7
Rice 18, 22, 30, 168–71
  Chicken Steamed with Rice
    in Lotus Leaves 120
  Egg-fried Rice 175
  Egg Fu Yung 177
  Eight-treasures Sweet Rice Cake 248
  Fried Rice with Pork and Shrimp 176
  Glutinous Rice 30, 234–7
  Hainan Chicken Rice 129
  Steamed White Rice 174
  Winter Rice Pudding with
    Dried Fruits 247
  Xinjiang Rice Pot with Lamb 158
Rice Noodles with Beef in
  Black Bean Sauce 192
Rock Sugar 23, 30

Saang Choi Baau 122
Salt-roasted Chicken 130
San Choy Bau 122
San Geung Yeung Naam Bou 157
San Geung Yeung Yuk Faan 158
Scallions 18, 31
  Sesame and Scallion
    Dipping Sauce 29
  Scallion Cakes 47
Scallops 79
  Scallops in Black Bean Sauce 102
  Stir-fried Scallops with Asparagus 100
  see *also* Conpoy
Scrambled Eggs with Beancurd 226
Sesame
  Chengdu Noodles in Sesame Sauce 182
  Oil 30
  Pastes 24, 30
  Sesame and Scallion
    Dipping Sauce 29
Seun Jim Dau Fu 225
Shaoxing Rice Wine 23, 31
Shrimp 79
  Dried Shrimp 29
  Drunken Shrimp 93
  Fried Rice with Pork and Shrimp 176
  Shrimp Fu Yung 96
  Shrimp Toasts 46
  Soft-wrapped Pork and Shrimp Rolls 44
  Wok-fried Jumbo Shrimp in Spicy Sauce
    99
Si Jap Chaau Dai Ji 102
Si Jap Chaau Hin 105
Si Jap Jin Taap Sa 92

Si Jiu Ngau Ho 192
Si Miu Baak Faan 174
Si Yau Gai Yik 56
Sichuan Fried Eggplant 208
Sichuan Peppers 24, 31
Sichuan Pickle 30
Sichuan Pumpkin Soup 67
Sing Dou Ma Laat Min 182
Sing Jau Chaau Mai 195
Singapore Noodles 195
Skins 31
Snow Peas
  Broccoli and Snow Pea Stir-fry 222
Soft-wrapped Pork and Shrimp Rolls 44
Sole
  Steamed Sole with Black Bean Sauce 92
Sou Choi Cheun Gyun 43
Soup 13, 24, 79
  Beancurd and Bean Sprout 61
  Crab and Corn 66
  Ground Beef and Cilantro 69
  Hot-and-sour 65
  Sichuan Pumpkin 67
  Tomato with Conpoy 70
  Whole Chicken 71
  Won Ton 72
Soy Mustard Dipping Sauce 29
Soy Sauce 18, 31
  Pork Ribs Braised in Soy Sauce 154
  Soy Chicken Wings 56
Soybeans 13, 21
  Marinated Soybeans 60
Spareribs in a Sweet-and-sour Sauce 152
Spicy Green Beans 212
Spicy Sichuan Pork 155
Spring Rolls 40
  Skins 31
  Vegetarian Spring Rolls 43
Squid
  Baby Squid Stuffed with
    Pork and Mushrooms 106
Star Anise 31
  Braised Beef with Star Anise 138
Steamed Sole with Black Bean Sauce 92
Steamed White Rice 174
Stir-fried
  Bean Sprouts 215
  Beef with Broccoli and Ginger 147
  Chinese Greens 220
  Fresh Crab with Ginger 103
  Long Beans with Red Bell Pepper 214
  Scallops with Asparagus 100
  Shredded Chicken with Celery 133
Stock 31
Stuffed Eggplant with Spicy Sauce 211

Sweet-and-sour Dishes 23
  Spareribs in a Sweet-and-sour Sauce 152
  Sweet-and-sour Chicken 134
Syun Laat Tong 65

Tangerine Peel 31
Tea-scented Eggs 58
Toffee Apple Slices 240
Tomato Soup with Conpoy 70
Tomatoes 13, 21, 22
  Chinese Tomato Salad 231
Tong Chou Paai Gwat 152

Vegetables 21, 22, 196–231
  Preserved 13, 24, 30
Vegetarian Spring Rolls 43
Vinegar 21, 23, 30

Waat Daan Dau Fu 226
Whitebait with Green Chili 57
Whole Chicken Soup 71
Wine 21, 23, 31
Winter Rice Pudding with Dried Fruits 247
Wok-fried Jumbo Shrimp in Spicy Sauce 99
Woks 28
Won Ton Soup 72
Wrappers 31
Wui Wo Yuk 155
Wun Teui Ching Gai Tong 71
Wun Tun Tong 72

Xinjiang Lamb Casserole 157
Xinjiang Rice Pot with Lamb 158

Yeung Jau Chaau Faan 176
Yip Guk Gai 130
Yiu Gwo Gai Ding 125
Yu Heung Ke Ji 208
Yu Pin Juk 62
Yu Yuk Yeung Laat Jin 90
Yui Chyu Faan Ke Tong 70
Yuk Si Lou Min 191